TIME MANAGEMENT FOR MOMS

5 PATHS TO CONQUER CHAOS, MAXIMIZE
PRODUCTIVITY, BALANCE YOUR SCHEDULE, AND
RECLAIM YOUR WELL-DESERVED 'ME' MOMENTS

JULIA RAY

CONTENTS

INTRODUCTION

A mother's time is like no other.

Every moment is unique, unpredictable, and unrepeated. Time management helps in navigating these swift currents with grace and poise.

You have probably found yourself in a situation where it feels like you're standing at the edge of a cliff, with the noise of crashing waves below and the wind ripping around you, threatening to knock you off balance at any moment. That's what being a modern mom feels like sometimes - a delicate balance on the precipice of chaos. Between gadgets and apps clamoring for our attention, planning a well-structured day, and the constant need to declutter and embrace minimalism, we face a cacophony of challenges daily.

You see, modern motherhood is like walking on a tightrope. On one side, you're battling the ever-present gadgets that promise to simplify our lives but sometimes complicate them. Conversely, you're wrestling with the need to plan and structure your days efficiently while leaving room for spontaneity and fun. Add to that the societal pressure to say 'yes' to every request, every commitment and the constant need to declutter both your physical and mental space; it's no wonder we often feel like we're on the brink of collapse.

As moms, time for ourselves is a luxury we can seldom afford. Every minute is precious between caring for our children, managing the household, juggling our careers, and trying to carve out a sliver of 'me' time.

We all want more than 24 hours in a day, but we should first ask ourselves how we can have a very productive and happy life within these 24 hours we already have. Same time - but a more satisfying life.

Do you ask yourself where the time flies? Are you constantly racing against the clock, trying to be everything for everyone but feeling like there's never enough time in a day? If your life as a busy mom feels like an endless juggling act, constantly leaving you overwhelmed and exhausted, this book is your lifeline. It's is for every mom who has ever felt overwhelmed, who has felt the guilt of being torn between work and family, who has yearned for a pause button to stop the world for a moment. It's for every mom who has skipped a meal to ensure her kids are fed and who has put off her own needs to cater to those of her family.

At first glance, it seems having a planner is the easiest way to start your time-management adventure, but, in reality, almost all of us started and quickly forgot our daily and weekly planners. The main goal is to understand why!

This is where I come in, as a writer, a friend, and someone who's been on the battlefield of time management, just like you, your guide on this adventure, Julia Ray.

As a mom of two adorable, vibrant, and incredibly energetic kids, a four-year-old who's just beginning to explore this big world and an eight-year-old who's taking on school challenges and learning what independence means I've been through the wringer, trying to juggle motherhood, work, personal time, and the myriad of other responsibilities that come my way. I've battled gadget addiction, struggled with poor planning, and fought hard against the temptation to fill my life and home with unnecessary clutter. I've learned some lessons, some the hard way, but each has helped shape the strategies and solutions I share in this book.

Over the years, I've navigated the stormy seas of motherhood, gathering a wealth of experience and strategies that I'm eager to share with you. But why should you listen to me?

As an author, my authority mainly stems not only from academic degrees or professional accolades but from the school of hard knocks - motherhood. I've been in the trenches of modern parenting, facing the challenges that most mothers today can relate to - gadgets sucking up our time, the constant drive to declutter, planning, learning to say no, and delegating.

THE DAYS WERE ROUGH before I had this newfound understanding of time management. I was overwhelmed by the constant push and pull of various responsibilities. I was plagued by the guilt of not spending enough quality time with my children, struggling with the influx of unnecessary items cluttering my home, and being unable to say 'no' to requests that drained me. My days were dictated by my tasks, not the other way around.

Then, I embarked on an adventure of change that involved understanding and confronting my time management issues head-on. And now, I am here to share this adventure and its revelations with you.

What makes this book the right choice for you? If you've ever felt overwhelmed by the juggling act of modern motherhood, this book is for you. If you've ever felt like you're running on a hamster wheel, constantly busy but have yet to really get anywhere, this book is for you. If you've ever wondered how some women seem to 'do it all' while you're struggling to keep your head above water, this book is for you.

This book is the culmination of years of personal experiences, failures, triumphs, and much learning. It's a blend of practical tips and reflective exercises that'll give you the tools to reclaim control over your time and, ultimately, your life. I hope that, through these pages, you'll find strategies that resonate with you, strategies that spark a change.

Apart from being a mom like you, I've also been an observer and a researcher. I've seen fellow moms as they grapple with the same challenges, and I've listened to their stories. I've seen the devastation gadgets and poor planning can bring into a family's life. I've witnessed the magic that decluttering and saying a firm 'no' can create. And yes, I've been in the trenches, living through these challenges myself.

One day, as I watched my four-year-old mimicking me, her tiny fingers swiping the air as if scrolling an invisible phone, it hit me. I needed to change, and I needed to help others change as well.

This realization catalyzed a transformation adventure that took me several years. I started researching, experimenting, and learning. I had conversations with experts and other moms. I learned about the psychology of habits, the benefits of minimalism, and the art of effective planning.

The knowledge I've accumulated isn't from some lofty academic tower; it's real, grounded in motherhood's gritty, joyful, and sometimes messy reality. It's the same reality you're living in right now, which will make my advice relatable and practical.

Why did you pick up this book? Was it a particularly exhausting day when you fell into bed, realizing you had spent more time scrolling through your phone than interacting with your kids? Or maybe it was the frustration of seeing your plans crumble due to poor scheduling? Whatever the catalyst, I want you to know that I understand and, more importantly, can help.

By the end of this book, I promise you a newfound perspective on what causes time waste and how to combat it effectively. You'll learn how to manage your time more efficiently, master the art of decluttering and minimalism, navigate the tricky waters of planning your day, week, and month, cultivate the power to say "no" when needed, and effectively delegate tasks.

You will learn to identify your time management problems and will be equipped with tangible solutions, exercises, charts, and resources to overcome them. Each chapter resonates with different struggles and offers a pathway to overcome these struggles on the adventure to productive time management. You might relate to one, a few, or all of them, but rest assured; you will walk away with a solid action plan.

This book is your roadmap to that life. Here's what you'll gain:

1. Strategies to tackle gadget addiction: Learn practical techniques to control the time spent on your phone and various apps, allowing you to focus on what truly matters and regain the time for true self-enrichment. We will talk about using technology to Your Advantage.

2. Tools to embrace minimalism: Discover how decluttering your space can lead to a decluttered mind and, ultimately, more time in your hands. Learn to set realistic goals in your decluttering process and achieve them. Get your family engaged in transforming your cluttered space into a beautiful oasis.

3. Techniques for effective planning and prioritizing: I'll guide you to create a balanced, structured plan that works for your unique situation as a mom. By putting it into action, you will gain control of your time. We will discuss Priority as the Key: What needs immediate attention, and what can wait a while? Learning to prioritize tasks can significantly unclutter your schedule and mind.

4. Wisdom to delegate: Get practical advice on delegating tasks in different scenarios and tips to do it effectively to get tons off your shoulders and reclaim your 'me' time. Delegation is an art! There's no rule that states you have to do it all. Enlist your partner, older children, or other family members to help with chores. It takes a village to raise a child, after all.

5. Empowerment to say 'No': Get hands-on exercises to practice the power of saying 'no.' It's not selfish; it's a necessity in your time management adventure. Learn to decline commitments that will push you over the edge. Remember, it's quality over quantity.

I have seen extreme transformations using the strategies I will share with you.

Imagine waking up to a day when you're not already feeling defeated by the thought of the endless tasks ahead. Instead of being your enemy, your gadgets are tools that help you stay organized. Your home is a haven of peace, devoid of the unnecessary clutter that often subconsciously feeds into your stress.

You've got a clear, achievable plan for your day, week, and month, which you can easily adjust according to your family's needs. You know when it's time to work, time to play with your kids, time to relax, and time for yourself.

You've mastered the art of saying 'no,' and it doesn't feel like a guilt trip. You've set your boundaries, and people respect them. The moments spent saying 'yes' to things that matter to you make your life rich and fulfilling.

You've learned to delegate tasks that others can manage, freeing up your time to focus on activities that demand your attention and those that bring you joy.

You're living your life, not just viewing others live theirs.

This can be your reality, and that's the transformation this book can bring to your life.

Time management isn't a skill that is honed overnight. It's a pathway, and this book is your guide, a companion that will accompany you in every step. It took me years to accumulate this knowledge, and now, I pass it on to you, hoping it'll empower you as much as it did me.

By the end of this pathway, I hope you will embrace the concept that while we can't control time, we can control how we interact with it.

That's what this book is all about. It's about giving you the tools, strategies, and insights to help you navigate the complexities of motherhood without losing sight of your own needs and desires.

Over the coming chapters, we'll dive into the lives of five real moms, each facing unique struggles, and learn from their experiences. We'll explore practical, effective methods that go beyond the usual time management advice, enabling you to reclaim control over your time, your choices, and, ultimately, your life.

Because remember, Mom, you're not in this alone. As Maya Angelou once said, "Each time a woman stands up for herself, without knowing it possibly, without claiming it, she stands up for all women." By choosing to manage your time, your way, you are not only improving your own life but also paving the way for other moms to do the same.

So, dear reader, consider this book your sign if you're looking for a sign that it's time to take back control of your time. As you turn these pages, remember that you're not alone in this struggle, and change, though challenging, is entirely within your reach. This is the right book for you; now is the perfect time to start. Welcome to our pathway together!

1

TURNING TECHNOLOGY INTO OUR FRIEND

EMILY'S STORY

"Life is what happens to us while we are making other plans."

— ALLEN SAUNDERS

This quote has always resonated with me, reminding me of the precious nature of time and how easy it can be to let it slip through our fingers. Here is a story about a friend of mine. Let's call her Emily, a brilliant woman who, much like myself, has struggled with this same concept.

Emily is a strong, incredibly devoted mother, like a symphony conductor orchestrating the vibrant rhythm of life for her two children, a boy of 7 and a girl of 11. Emily focused on nurturing her family, exchanging her professional aspirations for being a stay-at-home mom. She built a picture-perfect family, so it seemed on the surface. Yet, in the quiet moments, Emily confessed to me her growing sense of uneasiness, a restlessness churning beneath the surface.

It wasn't just the monotony of chores or the unending cycle of school runs, soccer practices, and violin lessons. No, Emily's struggle lay within her habits—habits deeply intertwined with technology.

Emily's story is quite inspiring, and it's something that can encourage us all.

It was a perfect Sunday morning. Emily woke up to the chirping birds, the sun peeping through the blinds, promising a beautiful day. She stretched lazily, planning an unhurried day with her kids, a quiet breakfast, maybe a trip to the park, and an afternoon of crafting or baking cookies. But something changed right after breakfast as she reached for her phone to check the time. One notification led to another, and the next thing she knew, the morning sun was replaced by the harsh afternoon light. She was lost, lost in a world within a five-inch screen, while her kids, their hope of a fun day with mom slowly fading, turned to their own devices.

Sounds familiar? It probably does because we've all been stuck in the vortex of gadgets and social media, losing track of our precious time. And in the process, we tend to lose sight of what's truly important: our real lives, our children, our passions, and even ourselves.

In the age of technology, we were promised the gift of time. Automatic washing machines, instant messaging, lightning-fast internet - all of these innovations were supposed to make life easier and free up our precious hours. Yet somehow, we find ourselves busier than ever. Instead of gaining time, it seems like we've just gained more things to do, more speed at which we must move, and more noise to filter through.

Let me share with you a stunning statistic. As per recent research by Steven Zauderer, around 70% of teens and young adults in the United States find themselves entangled in the labyrinth of social media addiction. This isn't just an issue confined to our youngsters. Over 50% of Americans aged between 30 and 49 are in the same trap. Now, pause and consider: The average person spends a staggering 1 hour and 40 minutes daily on social media. That's over 12 hours a week, more than half a day that could be spent doing something more meaningful or even just resting and recharging.

Isn't it ironic? The very tools that were designed to bring the world to our fingertips and save us time have ended up consuming it.

Consider this. Emily, like so many of us, carries her cell phone like a lifeline, constantly connected to the world. This small, handheld device became Emily's constant companion, her refuge in the rare quiet moments, her insomnia companion, and her unintentional time thief.

Day in and day out, Emily found herself engrossed in an unending stream of notifications, each one punctuating her time like a tick of a clock. The whirring world of social media and the allure of an 'always-on' lifestyle began to feel like an obligation, a demanding presence that insisted upon its attention.

And the impact? Emily confessed to the creeping sensation of not being entirely present. Her mind split between the reality around her and the digital world in her palm. I noticed it, too, the emotional disconnect subtly threading its way through Emily's interactions with her family and friends. Her children began to notice, their young minds mirroring their mother's actions, eyes on screens instead of each other.

Perhaps, as you're reading this, you see a bit of yourself in Emily, recognizing these habits as your own mirror. I certainly did. But don't despair; this is not a lamentation. Instead, it's a call to awareness and a call to action.

First and foremost, let's get one thing straight: technology is not the enemy. It's an incredible tool that, when used mindfully, can facilitate connections, foster learning, and help manage the many hats we wear as mothers. The problem isn't the tool but how we use it.

Now, I know change can feel daunting, especially when it involves breaking ingrained habits. So, let's take this step-by-step, starting with acknowledging the patterns that no longer serve us. Here are a few tech habits you might recognize:

1. Being always available.
2. Going to sleep with your phone.
3. Checking your phone first thing in the morning.
4. Eating as you work on a computer.

5. Texting over talking.
6. Using your smartphone as a social clutch.
7. Not taking a break from social media.
8. Letting the technological clutter win.

I am sure you recognize some, just like I did, and so did Emily. The first step is recognizing these habits, but the actual change comes in confronting them.

TECH CAN BE HELPFUL OR A WASTE OF TIME

"When time feels like a scarce commodity, remember the words of William Penn: 'Time is what we want most, but what we use worst.' A mother's talent for time management can turn this scarce commodity into a wellspring of productivity and tranquility."

Well, let's take a moment here. Consider how we've all come to rely on our smartphones, computers, tablets - you name it. In an age where the world is literally at our fingertips, the potential to access knowledge, connect with others, and manage our busy lives is indeed mind-boggling. But I think we can all agree that this digital ease also comes with its pitfalls.

I'm talking about those tiny pings that seem to draw our attention away at the most inopportune times. The unending scroll of social media feeds, the constant influx of emails, the ongoing need to check and respond. Suddenly, what should be a fantastic tool for efficiency and connectivity becomes a relentless distraction.

Let's look at this realistically. As moms, we are not just responsible for ourselves but also for our children. The world they are growing up in vastly differs from what we used to know. Technology is a significant part of their lives, and there's no turning back from that.

But here's the catch: the more we become engrossed in our digital worlds, the more our children seem to follow suit. Family time starts to feel like a gathering of tech zombies, everyone hunched over their own little screens, engrossed in a universe that doesn't involve human interaction. It sounds a bit grim.

And let's not forget the information overload. The internet is a fantastic resource, no doubt, but it's also a never-ending data vortex. As moms, we feel obligated to stay up-to-date with the latest trends, best practices, health tips, recipes, DIY hacks, and all other advice out there. This quest for knowledge can quickly become an all-consuming pathway that leaves us with a debilitating feeling of inadequacy and decision fatigue.

What about multitasking? Technology is often hailed as the ultimate enabler of multitasking, helping us juggle several things simultaneously. The reality? Our brains are not wired for efficient multitasking, especially when it involves complex tasks requiring attention. When we're constantly distracted by notifications or the temptation to check our devices, our productivity dips, and our stress levels rise. Not exactly the recipe for a peaceful, organized life, is it?

Then comes the darker aspect of our relationship with technology: addiction. It's a strong word, I know, but let's not mince words here. Studies show that excessive use of digital devices can lead to symptoms akin to other forms of addiction, including anxiety, depression, irritability, restlessness, and even ADHD. And that is not exactly the kind of mental state we want to cultivate as mothers.

Of course, I'm not suggesting we toss all our devices out the window and revert to carrier pigeons for communication. That's not realistic or desirable. However, I am suggesting we look closer at our relationship with technology and see it for what it truly is - a tool, not a master.

WHY DO WE DO IT?

"There's a time for everything and a season for every activity under the heavens," the famous Ecclesiastes verse goes. But where, oh where, is the season for mindless scrolling, binge-watching, or sinking hours into a video game? Funny how we don't remember reading about that in our holy books or wisdom traditions.

Yet here we are, living in a digital age where technology dictates our rhythms more often than we'd like to admit. We find ourselves sinking hours into screens, driven by this invisible force. Why do we do it? I can think of a few reasons, and perhaps you'll see a glimpse of your own experiences in them.

First, there's the undeniable allure of relaxation and escape that digital indulgences offer. Imagine this: You've just put the kids to bed, tidied up the kitchen, and finally have some time for yourself. The allure of settling down with a good Netflix series or diving into the world of social media is, at that moment, irresistible. And let's not forget the dopamine rush that keeps you glued to the screen, even as episode after episode plays on or the scroll seems endless. It's a slippery slope, and before you know it, this momentary escape can morph into a habit, even an addiction.

Then there's the 'always-on' mentality, the modern malaise of needing to be constantly connected and updated. The countless messages, emails, notifications—they're like digital ties that bind, and it's easy to feel like we're falling behind if we're not on top of them. It's as if our worth and efficiency as individuals, professionals, and even mothers are measured in our response times or digital presence.

Not to mention, our digital devices often double as security blankets. Whether we're waiting for the school bus, at the doctor's office, or even taking a few moments in the restroom (yes, we've all been there), we cling to our devices, seeking solace in the constant connection they provide. There's an illusion of productivity, of not wasting time, that can make these moments feel purposeful.

And lastly, we might be grappling with the habit of a scattered focus. Our digital age is a buffet of distractions. With so much vying for our attention, we've become accustomed to split concentration, multiscreen experiences, and jumping from one digital task to another. This habit, over time, can erode our ability to maintain a deep, sustained focus on a single task.

Indeed, I may have delineated a harsh reality, but bear in mind that identifying the problem is the cornerstone of bringing about change. I am here to reassure you that rewriting these digital behaviors is not only achievable, but within your grasp. The path may be demanding—it will call for deliberate actions, a generous dose of self-compassion, and certainly, time. Yet, isn't regaining our time and tranquility a worthy pursuit?

To wrap this up, let's consider how we can turn technology from an adversary to an ally, to regain control over our time. As we move forward, we'll look into various time management strategies that utilize technology to enhance our productivity and peace rather than diminish it.

TECH'S NEGATIVE IMPACT ON FAMILY RELATIONSHIPS

"Just as Jim Rohn once stated, 'Either run the day, or the day runs you.' Being proactive in managing your time can allow you to be the master of your day instead of feeling at its mercy."

Imagine sitting at a coffee shop, laptop open, sipping on a fresh cappuccino, and scrolling through your emails. You are no stranger to the countless wonders of technology - it helps you stay connected with your family and friends, keeps you up to date with the world, and even allows you to work from the comfort of your own home. But have you ever thought about the implications of technology on our mental and physical health? And even more so, on the health and well-being of our children?

If you're anything like me, you've probably found yourself checking your phone just a little too often, becoming lost in a whirlpool of social media, and suddenly realizing you've spent hours staring at a screen. We've all been there. Just like every other mom trying to juggle work, family, and personal life, I, too, have succumbed to the hypnotic trance of technology.

Here's a startling fact: recent studies suggest that overuse or dependence on technology can lead to adverse psychological effects, such as feelings of isolation, depression, and anxiety. Surprisingly ironic, isn't it? Social media platforms that were designed to bring us closer might actually create a chasm between us and the real world. But don't worry; you're not alone in this - it's a struggle that many of us face.

Physically, overusing technology can lead to many issues, such as eyestrain, poor posture, sleep problems, and even reduced physical activity. It's daunting, yes, but the key is to develop healthful habits that can help us balance our reliance on technology and the need for physical well-being.

And as a mother, our concerns multiply when it comes to our children. It's undeniable that technology plays a crucial role in the lives of our kids. However, it's important to acknowledge that overuse of technology may have even more significant impacts on developing children and teenagers. From low academic performance and lack of attention to physical inactivity and obesity, the potential negative effects are alarming.

While I paint quite a grim picture, don't let it overwhelm you. There is no need to eliminate technology from our lives completely - that would be as impractical as trying to stop the flow of a river. The solution lies in finding a balance, a way to navigate the inevitable technological world while ensuring it doesn't adversely affect our mental and physical health.

Consider integrating the 20-20-20 rule into your routine, to manage this delicate balance. For every 20 minutes of screen time, take a 20-second break to look at something 20 feet away. This little trick can reduce the strain on your eyes from prolonged screen time.

We can also explore other ways to create a healthier relationship with technology. For instance, instead of using electronic devices before bedtime, why not wind down with a good book, some light stretches, or even a warm, relaxing bath?

TECH ADDICTION: WILL WE KNOW?

"The biggest lie we tell ourselves is that we're just one more click away from bliss, or the answer, or something meaningful. But that's not how technology works, nor how happiness is found."

— CAL NEWPORT

I'm sure you've had one of those days. You know, when your to-do list is a mile long, the kids are a touch too hyper, and everything feels like it's been cranked up a few notches. So, you sit down for just a moment, a quick reprieve, and you find yourself reaching for your phone or opening your laptop. Before you know it, hours have passed by, your tasks remain undone, and that fleeting moment of 'me time' got sucked into the vortex of scrolling, liking, sharing, and repeating.

You might wonder, have I become addicted to technology? I've asked myself the same question on more than a few occasions.

It can be hard to admit, but sometimes we end up doing more harm than good when we lean on technology as an escape. We tell ourselves, "Just one more email," or "One more episode," or "One more scroll down Instagram," but in reality, we're just avoiding the chaos of our lives. And here's the kicker - we know it. We know it's not good for us, but we can't help it. It's like being on a riptide, struggling to swim against the current but gradually getting pulled deeper into the digital sea.

Think of those moments when you've hidden your screen from a loved one or downplayed the hours spent online. Do you ever feel like you're performing a digital juggling act, trying to balance real life with the enticing glow of the screen? It's a struggle familiar to so many of us. I've been there, wrestling with the feeling of being digitally overstretched and under-connected to my actual life.

Let's take a moment and ask ourselves honestly, is our digital consumption a tool for growth and connection, or is it a distraction, a crutch we lean on when reality feels over-whelming?

This realization is not meant to cast guilt or blame - quite the contrary. It's about awakening awareness and prompting action.

So, here's an exercise, a little 'reality-check' worksheet to help you understand your digital habits better:

1. How much time do you spend online each day?
2. What are the three apps or websites you spend most of your time on?
3. Do you find yourself reaching for your device when you're stressed or anxious?
4. Have you ever hidden your screen time or lied about it to someone close to you?
5. Do you feel restless or uneasy when you're away from your device for a prolonged period?

Take a moment to reflect on your answers. No judgments, just honesty. Are your habits serving you, or are they serving as a hurdle in your pursuit of a balanced, fulfilling life and your time management goals?

Remember, time is the most precious resource we have as moms and human beings. It's our duty to ourselves and our loved ones to ensure we're spending it wisely and not letting it slip away into the digital ether.

If you're anything like me, you've probably felt the cruel crunch of time. I see you, fellow mom, battling the clock, racing against the relentless seconds that seem to sprint when the to-do list is a mile long. We're standing shoulder to shoulder on the front-line, the battlefield that is our day-to-day life. As glorious as it is, motherhood comes with its fair share of chaos and time management struggles. Well, it's the sword we need to wield.

HOW EMILY OVERCAME HER TECH ADDICTION

"Technology can be our best friend, and technology can also be the biggest party pooper of our lives. It interrupts our own story, interrupts our ability to have a thought or a daydream, to imagine something wonderful, because we're too busy bridging the walk from the cafeteria back to the office on the cell phone."

— STEVEN SPIELBERG

The words of Spielberg echo in my mind as I think about Emily.

Emily, much like many of us, was tethered to her phone. It was as if her world orbited around her devices instead of the other way around. Between replying to emails, staying updated with her kids' school events, managing grocery lists on apps, and attempting to maintain some semblance of a social media presence, she was lost in a whirlwind of digital chaos.

She realized she had a tech addiction when one day, her seven-year-old asked her, "Mommy, why are you looking at your phone while I am trying to tell you about my new friend?" That question hit her like a lightning bolt. She knew things had to change, but where to begin? It seemed like an uphill task.

Her first step towards breaking this addiction was acknowledging it. She admitted that her tech use had spiraled out of control, affecting her relationships and, significantly, her time.

That admission was crucial because recognizing a problem is the first step in solving it.

Emily then adopted a tool that we all can easily implement - digital detox periods. She decided to switch off her devices for certain hours each day. This was challenging, but she kept her goal in mind. She strove for undisturbed quality time with her family.

She also brought about small changes in her routines. Instead of checking her messages first thing in the morning, she meditated. Instead of ending her day scrolling through social media, she switched to reading. These replacements were small yet significant steps in her tech-breakup pathway.

As time went by, Emily noticed something remarkable. She started feeling less anxious and less hurried, started discovering these beautiful pockets of time she never knew existed before. Furthermore, she had more time for herself, her kids, and the family, and felt happier.

Breaking free from her tech addiction was no easy feat for Emily. It took determination, courage, and consistency. But the result? Totally worth it.

Now, I'm not saying you should replicate Emily's actions down to the T. Her methods might not be your methods, and that's perfectly fine. The critical takeaway here is that you can overcome your tech addiction, just like Emily. You can reclaim your time, regain control of your life, and you don't have to do it alone. This book is here to guide you along that path, providing practical methods and insights derived from real-life stories just like Emily's.

To kickstart this pathway, I'd suggest a small exercise. Note down the amount of time you spend on your digital devices for a couple of days. Be honest with yourself. This will show you how deeply technology has permeated your daily routine. And remember, it's not about completely eliminating technology from our lives; it's about controlling it and using it as a tool for our benefit rather than letting it control us. And together, we can achieve this.

HOW WE CAN MAKE TECH OUR FRIEND INSTEAD OF OUR ENEMY

"There's a way to do it better - find it."

— THOMAS A. EDISON

As I reflect on Edison's words, they offer a gentle nudge, a whisper of reassurance. It's a reminder that even when we find ourselves tangled in our technology-led lives, there is always a way to untangle and improve.

Now, you may remember our chat about Emily and her pathway toward breaking her tech addiction. What stood out in her story was that she didn't renounce technology entirely, because, let's be honest, that's hardly practical in today's world.

Instead, Emily found ways to turn technology into an ally rather than an adversary. And believe me, if Emily could do it, you can too.

Firstly, it all starts with setting boundaries. I've found that keeping devices away from the bedside table works wonders. How many times have we all been guilty of ending our day with a screen-lit face, scrolling aimlessly until our eyes can no longer stay open? By keeping devices at bay, we give ourselves a chance to disconnect and allow our minds to wind down.

Also, taking tech "holidays" is something Emily found incredibly helpful. Select a day, perhaps over the weekend, when you consciously decide to keep your device usage to a minimum. You'd be amazed at the time you suddenly have at your disposal. The time that you can spend on hobbies, relaxation, or simply being present with your family.

The concept of having designated tech-free zones at home might initially seem unusual. But give it a try. Have areas where the emphasis is on interaction, conversation, or quiet contemplation. It sets a tone, a rhythm to our lives that isn't dictated by the ping of a notification.

It's a bit like those old-school movie nights, remember? We'd gather around the TV, popcorn in hand, and dive into a film together. That sense of shared experience is what we're aiming for here. Let's rekindle that tradition and keep the TV off at other times, encouraging more organic, in-person connections.

What about designating specific times to check messages and news? Instead of constantly being alert for the next update, choose certain slots in your day for this. Just ensure it's not the first thing in the morning or the last thing at night. Our minds are impressionable during these times, and starting or ending the day with potentially stress-inducing news isn't the best idea.

Now, here's a fun thing you could try. Incentivize yourself to stay away from your device for specific periods. You may put a dollar in a jar every hour you stay device-free. At the end of the month, use that money to pamper yourself. Who knew ignoring your phone could lead to a spa day?

Lastly, it's important to remember that seeking professional help is never a sign of weakness. Do not hesitate to get support if you believe your relationship with technology is edging towards addiction. There are numerous resources out there that can help, and you're not alone in this pathway. This is a marathon, not a sprint. It's about steady, consistent steps towards the goal of creating a balanced relationship with technology, where it serves us, not controls us.

Why not begin this pathway by trying one of the above methods this week? Or if you've got a unique method of your own, go ahead with that. Remember, this isn't about competition or comparison. It's about finding what works best for you, in your life, on your terms. Because at the end of the day, that's what time management is all about, isn't it? It's about creating a life that resonates with who we are and how we want to live.

SUMMARY

"As the ancient Chinese proverb goes, 'The best time to plant a tree was 20 years ago. The second-best time is now.' It's never too late to start taking control of your time and designing a life that embraces your motherhood and your individuality."

Welcome to the thrilling close of Chapter 1, where we've embarked on an eye-opening pathway following the story of Emily. Together, we've looked into the startling depths of technology addiction and its profound effects on personal life and relationships.

This chapter has raised the curtain on how technology, an entity intended to liberate us, can entangle us in a digital snare, robbing us of focus and stealing precious time. It provided striking statistics revealing that a significant portion of the US population, including teens, young adults, and adults across genders, are caught up in the web of social media addiction.

Our protagonist, Emily, found herself entangled in the same trap, allowing her tech habits to consume her daily life, impacting not just her sleep and mental wellbeing but also her ability to be present for her family. Her story tugged at our heartstrings, prompting us to reflect on our tech habits.

Unraveling the complexities of digital distractions, the chapter dove into how constant notifications, social media platforms, and the infinite flow of online information can lead to information overload, hinder productivity, and trigger mental health issues. Further, it addressed how the "always-on" mentality and the dopamine rush from binge-watching or mindless scrolling can turn technology into a security blanket rather than a mere tool.

But friends, don't despair! As we pathwayed through Emily's struggle, we also learned about her victorious battle against tech addiction, offering a ray of hope for anyone caught in this digital trap. With practical tips like keeping devices away from the bedside, taking tech holidays, designating tech zones and time slots, and seeking professional help if needed, we learned that turning tech from foe to friend is possible!

Now, equipped with these invaluable insights and ready to undertake a digital detox, we march on toward the next chapter, invigorated with the prospect of healthier tech habits and a renewed focus. Let's take these lessons to heart and remember to ask ourselves, "Are we using technology, or is it using us?"

WORKSHEET

Exercises:

1. Reflect on your tech habits. How much time do you spend scrolling through social media daily?

Notes:

....

....

2. What distractions does technology create in your life that impact your successful time management?

Notes:

....

....

3. How does your use of technology impact your time with family and relationships?

Notes:

....

....

4. What are some signs that you may be addicted to technology?

Notes:

....

....

5. Think of ways to turn tech into your friend rather than your foe. List them below.

Notes:

Practice Questions:

1. How does technology use contribute to your time management decision paralysis?

2. How can technology promote multitasking inefficiency?

3. Why do people resort to binge-watching, scrolling, or gaming?

4. How does technology addiction affect one's relationship with time management?

5. How can designated tech-free areas in the home help manage technology usage?

Frequently Asked Questions:

1. How can technology negatively impact family time and relationships?

2. Why is it important to keep devices away from our bedsides?

3. What are the signs of technology addiction?

4. How can technology serve as a tool rather than a time waster?

5. How can taking tech "holidays" help improve our relationship with technology and our time management skills?

Table:

Technology Habits	Impact on Life	Possible Solutions

Key Takeaways:

1. Overuse of technology can lead to loss of focus and time wastage.

Notes:

_____

_____

2. Technology addictions can have severe impacts on mental health and family relationships.

Notes:

_____

_____

3. Unhealthy tech habits can be broken with concerted effort and the right strategies.

Notes:

_____

_____

4. Technology can serve as a helpful time management tool when used effectively and in moderation.

Notes:

_____

_____

5. Taking tech "holidays", designating tech areas, and specific times to check messages can help manage technology usage and improve your time management.

Notes:

_____

_____

Action Steps:

1. Begin by assessing your current technology usage habits and their impact on your life and your time management.

_____

_____

2. Identify areas where technology is more of a distraction than a tool.

----

3. Set clear boundaries for your technology use, such as tech-free zones and times.

----

4. Implement a consistent plan for reducing unnecessary technology use and stick to it.

----

5. Seek professional support if you find it challenging to manage your technology usage on your own.

EMBRACING MINIMALISM

SARAH'S STORY

Have you ever found yourself holding the fort, juggling every imaginable responsibility, with hardly a moment to breathe? I bet you have because we've all been there. Let me share the story of a friend of mine, Sarah.

Sarah is an easygoing, charming lady. She is a third-grade teacher at school, and her class adores her. She is also a mom of a fun-loving 13-year-old son. Like most boys his age, he has lots of dreams and an always-hungry stomach. His laughs and funny actions bring joy to their big home. Sarah's husband is a truck driver — a kind man who cares much about his family. However, his work keeps him away for weeks, so often Sarah has to take care of everything at home on her own.

Sarah is a woman who appreciates what she has in life and takes pride in having a loving husband, a wonderful son, and a comfortable, spacious home. Yet, there's a story to tell about Sarah. At times being overwhelmed with loads of school papers piling on her desk, a sink of dirty dishes, and her son's teenage friends having the time of their lives in her house, leaving a mess after themselves, Sarah needs a break, she needs to recharge, and she fills her time with shopping. She loves to shop, maybe a bit too much. The word "Sale" is simply irresistible for her.

She started to escape the everyday routine by buying stuff they didn't really need, stuff that did not bring any value into their lives. This shopping habit has created a big mess in her house and her time management goals.

Being a teenager, her son did not understand the clutter problem. Getting him to clean up after himself was tough, let alone organize the clutter created by all the knickknacks and extras in their house. Sarah started feeling that instead of enjoying her beautiful spacious home, she often finds herself in a cluttered home with a big shopping problem.

Sarah was busy. Not just 'I-have-a-lot-to-do' busy, but 'there-aren't-enough-hours-in-the-day' kind of busy. The dishes piled up, the laundry seemed to multiply on its own, and somewhere amidst the chaos, Sarah was trying to find time to help her son with his homework and make him healthy meals. Tidying the house often took a backseat. As Sarah's story unfolds, you may see a little bit of yourself in her. You may recognize her struggles, her triumphs, and defeats because they're so common in our lives as mothers.

The state of Sarah's home began to affect her family life. The clutter wasn't just physical; it crept into their lives, causing stress and anxiety. Her son couldn't find his school assignments in the pile of papers on the dining table. Sarah often found herself rushing to find a clean shirt for her son in the early morning chaos. Clearly the clutter was taking over, affecting their well-being and their relationships.

Now, this isn't about shaming Sarah. On the contrary, it's about empathizing with her. She was doing the best she could with the circumstances she was in. She was a mother, a wife, a home-maker, a teacher, all rolled into one, trying to run the show as best she could. She was living the story of millions of moms out there, and maybe your story too.

We all have our 'clutter habits,' whether it's piles of unsorted mail, dishes in the sink, or toys scattered around the house. It may seem harmless, but clutter has a sneaky way of consuming our energy and time. When you're scrambling to find your child's lost shoe in a sea of toys or rummaging through a pile of papers for an unpaid bill, you are losing valuable time — time you could have spent on yourself or with your family.

So, how did Sarah fight the clutter?

It wasn't easy, and it didn't happen overnight. It began with small changes, little habits formed over time, slowly trans- forming her home and her life. She reconsidered her shopping habits, tackled one area at a time, and slowly, she began to feel lighter, happier, and more in control of her space and time.

This is Sarah's story, but it's not just her story. It's a tale that echoes in homes around the world. Your home may not be picture-perfect, and that's okay. We're not striving for perfection here; we're striving for better; better management of our time, better organization of our spaces, and ultimately, a better, happier life for us and our families.

HOW CLUTTER IMPACTS YOUR LIFE

"We don't need to increase our goods nearly as much as we need to scale down our wants. Not wanting something is as good as possessing it."

— DONALD HORBAN

Have you ever wondered how a cluttered environment might affect your time, mental state, and even your relationships? Take a step back, and let's explore this together.

Remember Sarah, our friend with her son and her truck-driver husband? Let's take a deeper dive into how clutter impacted her daily life.

Sarah often found herself late. Why? Because she'd spend so much time looking for things. Misplaced keys, the missing shoe, the paperwork she swore was right there on the table. Each lost item became a time-stealing adventure. It's like that with clutter. It creates an obstacle course of stuff that you need to navigate around every day. The time you lose can never be regained.

But it wasn't just the time. It was the mental toll it took on her as well. Clutter isn't just physical; it's psychological. For Sarah, the constant visual reminder of the disorder was mentally draining. It's like having a hundred tiny, incomplete tasks screaming for attention. Each piece of clutter was a to-do list item she hadn't yet checked off, causing her stress levels to rise. She was tired, and constantly feeling overwhelmed. Her home, which should have been her sanctuary, became a source of anxiety.

And, of course, this didn't just affect Sarah, but her relationships as well. That cluttered environment created a ripple effect, impacting her son and husband. There was tension in the air; the disorder had silently crept into their shared spaces, disrupting harmony and fueling frustration. Misplaced items led to unnecessary conflicts. Missed school deadlines became a source of guilt, and the home environment felt more chaotic than calm.

Now let's bring this into your world. Look around. Do you see your own version of Sarah's clutter? How is it affecting your time, your mental state and your relationships?

Please take a moment and think about it. What could you accomplish with the time you spend looking for lost items? How much calmer would you feel if you weren't constantly reminded of tasks left undone? What if your home was a place of peace, a haven from the outside world for you and your family?

Here's a little task for you. Write down one area of your home that feels particularly cluttered. It could be your kitchen counter, desk, or your kids' play area. Note down how much time you spend cleaning or navigating that area, how it makes you feel, and how it affects your interaction with your family. Over the next few weeks, we'll revisit this note and see how small, consistent changes can transform that space and, by extension, your life.

HOW SARAH DECLUTTERED HER HOME

"You can't reach for anything new if your hands are still full of yesterday's junk."

— LOUISE SMITH

Now, let's rewind a bit and remember our friend Sarah. As we already know, clutter had taken over her life, time, and even her relationships. But she didn't let it define her story. She decided to change the narrative. She decided to declutter.

The very first thing she did was to set realistic goals. Rome wasn't built in a day, and a cluttered home can't be decluttered in one, either. Sarah knew she had to tackle this beast bit by bit. She decided to start with the family room, the heart of their home, where most of the chaos was centered. She gave herself two weeks to declutter this one room.

Sarah quickly realized that to declutter successfully, she needed a system that worked for her and her family. She decided to use the Four-Box Method: a box for trash, a box for giveaway, a box for keep, and a box for relocate. This simple sorting system helped her make quick decisions and kept her focused on the task at hand.

But Sarah was a mom, which meant she didn't just have her own clutter to deal with, but her family's as well. So, she came up with a fantastic idea: declutter baskets. She got a basket for each family member and labeled it with their name. Any item that belonged to that person and was found out of place went into the basket. It was then their responsibility to empty their basket at the end of the day. This not only helped with the clutter, but also taught her son the importance of picking up after himself.

Sarah also adopted a simple yet effective habit: she would never leave a room without carrying something to put away. This meant that every time she moved from one room to another, she took a small step towards decluttering.

However, one of the most impactful changes she made was deciding to put things in the right place the first time. She realized that most of the clutter was due to postponing this one simple task. Instead of putting the mail on the kitchen counter 'for now', she'd sort it right away. Instead of leaving the dishes in the sink 'for later', she'd wash them right after use. This one change made a huge difference in maintaining a clutter-free home.

Realizing that her innocent shopping habits became an obstacle on her path to a clutter-free home, Sarah started looking for other ways to channel her energy and started painting. She found a great new way to express herself. She found fulfillment in the quiet 'me' moments. This simple change had a tremendous effect on her time management.

And now, it's your turn. You've heard Sarah's story. You've seen how she turned her cluttered chaos into an orderly oasis. Let's create your decluttering plan. Take that area of your home you noted earlier, and let's apply Sarah's techniques.

1. Set a realistic goal: How long will you give yourself to declutter this area? Remember, it's not a race. The goal is progress, not perfection.

2. Find a system that works for you: Will you use the Four-Box Method or something else? Write down your chosen method.

3. Decide on a family decluttering strategy: How will you involve others in this process if you live with others? Will you use declutter baskets or another technique?

4. Make a commitment: Will you adopt Sarah's habit of never leaving a room without carrying something to put away? If not, what commitment are you willing to make?

5. Put things in the right place the first time: This may seem small, but it's a game-changer. Make a commitment to do this for one week and see the difference it makes.

SCHEDULE TIME FOR DECLUTTERING

Isn't it peculiar how we can find time to be overwhelmed by the clutter in our lives, but we claim we can't find the time to tackle it? It's like that junk drawer we all have. You know the one I'm talking about. That drawer where everything that doesn't have a home ends up. Every time you open it, you cringe. You know you need to clean it out. You even want to clean it out. But do you? Most likely, the answer is no.

But why?

Why do we let the clutter continue to pile up, continue to invade our space, our peace, our time? Well, it's because we think we don't have the time to deal with it. But here's the secret: You do have the time. You just need to make it.

That's what scheduling time for decluttering is all about. It's about making time for what matters - and decluttering matters. It matters more than you may realize.

Decluttering is not just about cleaning up your physical space. It's about freeing up your mental space. It's about eliminating those nagging tasks in the back of your mind. It's about reducing the amount of time you spend searching for your keys, your phone, your sanity.

So, how do you find the time to declutter? You schedule it.

Now, I know what you're thinking: "Schedule more things? Isn't that just adding to the chaos?" But trust me, scheduling time for decluttering is the key to conquering the chaos.

Here's how you do it:

1. First, you need to decide when you can start decluttering. It could be first thing in the morning when you're fresh and energized. It could be during nap time when the house is quiet. It could be after the kids are in bed and you can have some uninterrupted time to yourself. Pick a time that works best for you and stick to it.

2. Next, you need to decide how much time you are going to spend decluttering. Maybe you can only spare 15 minutes a day. That's okay. It's not about the quantity of time you spend decluttering; it's about the consistency. If you declutter for 15 minutes daily, by the end of the week, you will have spent almost two hours decluttering. That's a lot of progress!

3. Then, you need to decide what you will declutter. You could start with that dreaded junk drawer or tackle the kids' toy room. Maybe you brave the basement. It doesn't matter where you start. What matters is that you start.

4. Finally, you need to put it in your calendar. Just like you schedule doctors' appointments or parent-teacher conferences, you must schedule your decluttering sessions. Make it a non-negotiable appointment with yourself.

DONATE OR SELL ITEMS YOU NO LONGER NEED

Let's do a little experiment: Close your eyes and imagine a space in your home. Maybe it's that overflowing linen closet or the garage that's seen better days. Picture all the items you haven't touched, looked at, or even thought about in the past year. How does that make you feel? If your mental walkthrough left you feeling more stressed than serene, I've got good news: there's a simple solution, and it's called purging.

Ah, purging. It's such a beautiful word. It's like a deep exhale, a freeing of the unnecessary, a triumphant reclaiming of space. But for many of us, it's also a daunting word. It's linked with making decisions, letting go, and, most importantly, time — something we moms often find in short supply.

But let me assure you, taking the time to donate or sell items you no longer need is worth every moment invested. Each unused, unnecessary item in your house is a tiny thief. It steals your space, time, and even your peace of mind. With each item you purge, you're not only reclaiming your physical surroundings but also giving yourself a mental breather.

So, how do you get started? Well, let's walk through it together.

Firstly, determine what you're ready to let go of. Consider the usefulness of each item. Is it serving a purpose, or is it just collecting dust? If it's the latter, it might be time to part ways. And remember, your trash could very well be another person's treasure.

Now, onto the next step, decision-making: to sell or to donate?

Selling items is an excellent way to generate extra cash. Try local consignment shops, online platforms like eBay, or even a good old-fashioned yard sale. But keep in mind selling takes time and effort, so be sure it's worth it.

Donation, on the other hand, is usually a quicker process. Plus, it has the added bonus of helping others. Shelters, charities, and non-profits are always in need of items, and you'll get a warm fuzzy feeling knowing you've made a difference.

GET THE WHOLE FAMILY INVOLVED

Imagine this: You're standing in the middle of a mountain of laundry, your eldest is asking for help with homework, and your youngest is refusing to eat dinner. Sounds like a regular Tuesday evening, right? Amid this chaos, you wonder, 'Isn't there a better way?'

The answer is yes, there is a better way, and it involves everyone in your house. Because you know what? You're not alone in this and don't have to do it all by yourself.

Let's pause for a moment and rethink the family dynamic. Why should you carry all the weight? Your family is a team, and every team member has a role to play, abilities to contribute, and tasks they can be responsible for.

So, the secret is to get the whole family involved. Let each family member do what they are good at and what they can. You might be surprised by the hidden talents and untapped capabilities that lie within your household.

Your teenager may have a knack for organizing, and your youngest is fascinated by sorting out laundry colors. Let them! Give them time-framed tasks that are manageable and age-appropriate. The beauty of this approach is twofold: firstly, the work gets divided, making it lighter on everyone and helping you get more time on your hands. Secondly, your kids learn the value of contribution and responsibility.

The key to making this work is choice. People are more likely to commit to tasks they've chosen themselves. So, sit everyone down, discuss what needs to be done, and let them pick their tasks. This process will give them a sense of ownership and responsibility, making it more likely they will stick to it.

This is all about setting a new norm where everyone helps out and no one is left feeling overburdened. In this norm, helping becomes an expected part of being in the family, not an extra or an imposition.

To help you get started on this, I've put together a task assignment table. It's a simple tool to list down tasks, who is responsible, and their deadlines. You can place it on the fridge, or anywhere everyone can see it.

Remember, change takes time, and it might be a bit messy at the start. But don't lose heart. Keep reminding yourself and your family of the bigger picture: a home where everyone shares the load, where everyone contributes, and where you get to reclaim a bit more of your time.

It's a team effort, after all. Your family works together to create a clutter-free home where each individual's strength benefits everyone. Now isn't that a vision worth striving for?

TAKE BABY STEPS - TAKE YOUR TIME

Ah, the allure of the dramatic transformation, the complete overhaul. We've all been there. You've seen a picture of a spotless, color-coordinated pantry on Instagram and think, "Right, that's it! Tomorrow, my entire house will look like that!" But then reality sets in. The kids need attention, work deadlines loom, dinner isn't going to cook itself, and that pristine pantry quickly becomes a distant, unattainable dream.

But what if I told you that you don't need to achieve picture-perfect in one day or even one week? What if I said that the real magic lies in baby steps?

Let's take a breath and step back from the edge of grandiose ambitions. Picture-perfect is a lovely ideal, but it's often not realistic, especially when you're juggling a myriad of responsibilities. But here's the beautiful part: you don't need to be perfect, and you don't need to do it all at once.

Baby steps are your friend, your ally in the fight against chaos and clutter. Baby steps mean breaking down a massive task into manageable chunks, into steps so small that they almost seem too easy. It's about taking your time and allowing yourself to move at your own pace.

Today, you can sort out just one shelf in the pantry. That's a win. Tomorrow, you tackle a drawer in your kid's room.

Another win. By taking baby steps, you chip away at the problem bit by bit, and before you know it, you've made significant progress.

To help you with this, I suggest creating a simple task list of baby steps. For each area you want to organize, jot down all the little tasks it involves. This could be as simple as 'Sort canned goods' or 'Fold and arrange t-shirts in the drawer.' Stick this list somewhere you'll see it often, and tick off tasks as you complete them. Seeing your progress visualized will give you a motivational boost.

Remember, this is not a race. It's okay if life gets in the way sometimes. What matters is consistency, perseverance. It's about coming back to your list, to your baby steps, whenever you can.

The goal here isn't to achieve that Instagram-worthy pantry overnight; it's about gradually creating a more organized, less chaotic environment that works for you as well as developing new habits. It's about less time wasted searching for that elusive can of beans and more time spent doing what you love with the people you love.

HOW TO STOP THE CLUTTER FROM CREEPING BACK

"Clutter is nothing more than postponed decisions."

— BARBARA HEMPHILL

Let me paint a familiar picture. After weeks or even months of chipping away at the clutter around your house, donating, organizing, and cleaning, you've finally achieved a semblance of the order you dreamt about. You might even bask in the glory of your accomplishment, admiring the neat spaces and promising yourself to maintain this new-found serenity.

But then, life happens.

Kids happen. Work happens. And somehow, little by little, the clutter starts to creep back in. A sea of papers slowly engulfs the once-clear tabletop. The toys you neatly organized are strewn about the room again. That perfect pantry? Well, let's not even talk about that.

Clutter creep, as I like to call it, is a common phenomenon, especially when we're juggling so many roles and responsibilities. It's like that stubborn weed that keeps popping up no matter how often you pluck it out. So how do we combat this insidious invader? How do we stop the clutter from slowly taking over again?

Well, the first step is awareness. Often, clutter creep is a silent intruder. It happens so gradually that we hardly notice until we're knee-deep in chaos again. Make a conscious effort to observe your spaces. Regularly evaluate your living areas, especially those notorious for accumulating clutter.

Then comes the action. Try to cultivate the habit of immediate decision-making. Remember Hemphill's quote? Clutter is postponed decisions. So, let's stop postponing. When you bring something new into your home, decide right away where it belongs. When you're done using an item, put it back immediately where it's supposed to be. This way, you're nipping clutter creep in the bud.

Next, consistency. Incorporate regular decluttering into your schedule. It could be 15 minutes every day or an hour every weekend—whatever works for you. Regular decluttering sessions help you keep on top of things and prevent clutter from piling up.

Finally, remind yourself of your 'why'. Why did you declutter in the first place? Was it to create a peaceful environment for your family? Was it to save time and reduce stress? Whenever you're feeling overwhelmed or unmotivated, remember your why.

To help you with this process, I would like to offer a simple worksheet. It'll guide you in observing your spaces, making decisions, scheduling decluttering, and defining your 'why'. It's a simple tool, but I've found it can make a world of difference. The fight against clutter creep is ongoing, but with awareness, action, consistency, and your powerful 'why', you're more than equipped to keep it at bay. Remember, it's not about creating a picture-perfect home; it's about creating a home that serves you, where you can live with greater ease and joy. So go on, arm yourself with these strategies, and reclaim your space from the claws of clutter creep.

A SIMPLE DECLUTTERING ACTION PLAN

The magic of simplicity! If you've ever basked in the tranquility of a decluttered space, you know what I'm talking about. The air feels lighter, your mind feels clearer, and suddenly, everything seems a little less chaotic, doesn't it? But getting there, now that's where the real challenge lies. You stare at the piles of stuff around your house, and you're just not sure where to begin. I get it; I've been there.

What you need is an action plan, a road map that guides you through the cluttered landscape of your home, helping you navigate and conquer one space at a time. And not just any plan. You need a plan that's straightforward, flexible, and specifically designed for the busy mom's lifestyle. A plan that acknowledges and accommodates the interruptions and unpredictability that come with the territory of motherhood.

Well, you're in luck! Because right here, we're going to create that plan. A simple, adaptable decluttering action plan that you can tailor to your unique situation. Ready? Let's dive in!

Step 1: Identify Your Clutter Zones

Start by listing down all the areas in your house that need decluttering. Be specific. Instead of "kitchen," write "kitchen drawers," "kitchen countertop," "under the kitchen sink." Break it down.

Step 2: Prioritize

Next, rank these clutter zones based on how much their clutter affects your daily life. The playroom that's always a landmine of toys? Probably a high priority. The guest room that's turned into a storage unit? Maybe not as high.

Step 3: Set a Timer

Decide how much time you can realistically dedicate to decluttering each day. Even 15 minutes a day can make a significant difference. The key is consistency.

Step 4: Match Zones with Time Slots

Now, estimate how much time you'll need for each clutter zone. Match each zone with an appropriate number of your decluttering time slots. For example, if you can give 15 minutes a day, and you estimate the kitchen drawer will take an hour, that's four time slots.

Step 5: Create Your Schedule

Assign your clutter zones to your available time slots in order of priority. Write it down. Visualize your path.

Step 6: Get to Work and Track Your Progress

Start working on your plan. Cross off each completed zone for a satisfying visual of your progress.

Step 7: Celebrate and Maintain

Celebrate each victory, no matter how small. Maintaining your decluttered spaces is a path in itself. Devise simple systems that will help you keep clutter at bay.

You see, decluttering doesn't have to be this daunting task looming over your head. By breaking it down and tackling it bit by bit, you're creating an environment of success. It's not about marathon decluttering sessions that leave you drained. It's about consistent, manageable steps leading to sustainable change.

SUMMARY

As we close Chapter 2, we bid farewell to our Sarah, whose transformational path from chaos to calm has been truly inspiring. A hardworking mom with a truck-driver husband, Sarah's story underscored the reality many of us face - life is busy, clutter accumulates, and it can wreak havoc on our homes, minds, and relationships.

You're not alone if you've ever felt stressed or overwhelmed by the disorder in your home. We spend days of our lives in combined time just looking for lost items. Imagine what you could do with that time if you had it back!

Sarah's story was a living testament to this struggle, reminding us that clutter isn't just about stuff - but our time, mental state, and relationships. But more importantly, it taught us that decluttering is more manageable than it seems. With realistic goals, a functional system, and some commitment, we can reclaim control over our spaces and our lives.

Step by step, we followed Sarah as she transformed her home. We cheered her on as she implemented handy strategies like declutter baskets, putting things away properly the first time, and getting the whole family involved. We witnessed the impact of time-bound tasks and allowing people to contribute in ways they excel at. From donating or selling items to scheduling decluttering time, every method used was a testament to the power of practicality and persistence.

But Sarah's path didn't stop there. She showed us that keeping the clutter from creeping back in is an ongoing process, a life-style change that requires mindfulness and vigilance.

The beauty of this chapter is that it didn't just tell Sarah's story. It provided you, the reader, with the tools and strategies you need to continue on your own decluttering path. With the simple action plan provided, you're armed and ready to conquer the clutter in your own home.

Time management and organization go hand in hand, impacting not only our productivity but also our mental well-being. This chapter offers a comprehensive understanding of the connection between decluttering our physical spaces and freeing up mental resources, leading to more efficient use of time.

Decluttering doesn't simply mean getting rid of possessions but involves intelligently organizing our space to reflect our priorities and goals. This targeted approach to decluttering can improve focus, increase productivity, and reduce stress, ultimately leading to better time management.

When our environment is uncluttered, our minds can process information more effectively. We spend less time searching for things, being distracted, and feeling overwhelmed. This naturally frees up more time for activities that align with our goals and values.

I hope you found the actionable strategies on how to incorporate decluttering into your everyday routine without it becoming a daunting task and the chapter helped you learn to recognize clutter, make effective decisions about your family belongings, and maintain an organized living and working environment.

Just remember - it's about taking baby steps and doing what works for you and your family. It's about making tidiness and organization the new norm. It's about not just decluttering your home but decluttering your life.

In conclusion, decluttering is not just about physical cleanliness but also about mental clarity. It's a critical tool in managing our time more efficiently, leading to increased productivity, satisfaction, and, ultimately, more time for what truly matters to us.

WORKSHEET

Exercises:

1. Reflect on your personal clutter habits. How do these habits impact your daily life, relationships, and your time management? Write down examples that come to mind.

Notes:

_____

_____

2. Set three realistic goals for decluttering your space. What can you accomplish in a week? A month? A year?

Notes:

_____

_____

3. Brainstorm a system that could help you declutter and maintain order in your space. What are some strategies that could work for you and your family?

Notes:

_____

_____

4. Using the strategies that worked for Sarah, draft an initial decluttering action plan for yourself. How can you apply her strategies to your situation?

Notes:

Practice Questions:

1. Why did Sarah need to declutter her home?

2. What strategies did Sarah employ to declutter her home effectively?

3. How did clutter impact Sarah's life, especially her time and mental state?

4. How did Sarah involve her family in the decluttering process?

5. How did decluttering her space change Sarah's life and relationships?

_____

_____

Frequently Asked Questions:

1. Why is it essential to declutter one's space?

_____

_____

2. How can decluttering your space improve your mental health?

_____

_____

3. How to maintain a decluttered space over time?

_____

_____

4. Can decluttering have a positive impact on relationships and time management?

_____

_____

5. What strategies can I use to involve my family in decluttering activities?

_____

_____

Table:

Sarah's Decluttering Steps	How It Helped Her	How It Can Help You
Set realistic goals	Focused her efforts	Allows structured progress
Established a system	Increased efficiency	Cuts down on decision-making time
Used declutter baskets	Simplified organization	Easy visual reminder
Didn't leave a room empty-handed	Maintained cleanliness	Keeps clutter from building up
Put things in the right place	Avoided misplacement	Saves time finding items

Key Takeaways:

1. A cluttered house equals a cluttered mind. Simplifying your space can bring peace and clarity.

Notes:

_____

_____

2. Involving family in the decluttering process not only eases your burden but also encourages collective responsibility.

Notes:

_____

_____

3. Setting realistic goals and developing a system can make decluttering more manageable and effective.

Notes:

_____

_____

4. Keeping clutter under control requires consistent effort and small daily actions.

Notes:

_____

_____

5. Maintaining a decluttered home positively impacts time management, mental health, and relationships.

Notes:

_____

_____

Action Steps:

1. Identify one area of your space that you want to declutter first.

_____

_____

2. Write down a list of clutter habits you want to change.

3. Plan a decluttering schedule that works for you and your family.

4. Set up a system for maintaining a decluttered space (like declutter baskets).

5. Share your decluttering goals with your family and discuss how they can contribute.

PLANNING AND PRIORITIZING

Have you ever felt like a ship at sea, swayed and buffeted by winds and currents, with no idea of the course you're sailing? Ever wondered if the choices you make on a daily basis really align with what you want in life? Oh, I bet you have. We've all been there. All feeling the push and pull of expectations, responsibilities, and those little lists of to-dos that never seem to get to-done.

Let me introduce you to Jessica, one of us, one of the millions of moms in the world trying to do their best. Jessica is a mom of three rambunctious kids, all under the age of ten. Her life was a flurry of activity, from school drop-offs to grocery runs and back to cooking dinner, all in a day's work. And amidst all this, she worked alongside her partner in a high-powered corporate finance job.

You might think Jessica had it all together, perfectly juggling her commitments. But on the inside, it was a different story. The constant humming of her mind trying to keep track of all tasks, big or small, was like an orchestra without a conductor. Every single item in her life, from sending work emails to ensuring her youngest had his favorite socks clean for soccer practice, all seemed equally important. She ran tirelessly on this hamster wheel, barely managing to keep up, let alone get ahead.

Despite her busy life, Jessica was frequently frustrated by a nagging feeling that she wasn't spending her time where it mattered most. She often found herself lost in her work, missing out on those precious moments with her family. Her kids were growing up too fast, their giggles and antics fleeting, while she was buried in her laptop screen, forever chasing deadlines.

Her inability to prioritize was impacting her family and taking a toll on her health. She was too busy to care for herself, constantly pushing her needs and wants to the bottom of the list. Exercise, hobbies, and even just a few minutes of peace with a warm cup of coffee in the morning were luxuries she felt she couldn't afford.

The more Jessica tried to take care of everyone and everything else, the more she lost herself in the process. With her energies spread thin and her spirit wearied, it wasn't too long before the cracks began to show. But it was these cracks that would soon be her saving grace.

The answer wasn't to do more, but to do less, to do what mattered. But how could she determine what that was?

WHAT DOES A LACK OF PRIORITIES MEAN?

Alright, let's roll up our sleeves and talk priorities. You see, without clear priorities, everything seems important, and that's where the chaos starts. It's like trying to swim through a whirlpool when we don't have our priorities straight. We're just swept along, trying to keep our heads above water without making any real progress.

Consider our lifestyle choices. When we fail to establish what truly matters to us, we end up compromising our own health, happiness, and even our core values. We might skip meals or cancel that yoga class we've been looking forward to all week simply because we haven't classified them as a priority. But let me tell you, self-care isn't a luxury, it's a necessity. Just like the oxygen mask on a plane, we need to secure ours first before we can assist others.

Then there's the workload. It's like that pile of laundry that just keeps growing. The more we try to tackle it all at once, the more overwhelmed we feel. Instead of everything being a 'must do', we need to differentiate the 'need to do' from the 'nice to do'. Trust me, once you get into that mindset, that pile starts to look less like a mountain and more like a molehill.

And don't get me started on stress levels. Without clear priorities, we're like a ship lost at sea, being tossed about by every wave that comes our way. From the moment we open our eyes to the moment we fall asleep, our minds are filled with a constant barrage of tasks, decisions, and demands. It's exhausting and, frankly, not sustainable.

You see, a lack of priorities is a hidden danger. It's like walking on a path littered with landmines, not knowing which step might set one off. It's an invisible enemy, slowly eating away at our time, peace of mind, joy, and even health. We might not see it, but we can definitely feel it. And let me assure you, it's not just a 'mom thing'. It's a 'human thing'. We all face it, and we all have to find a way to navigate through it.

But don't despair. There's always light at the end of the tunnel. It all starts with setting clear priorities, letting go of what isn't serving us, and focusing on what truly matters. It's about making conscious decisions, like carving out time for self-care, setting boundaries, and learning to say 'no' when needed.

HOW DO YOU KNOW IF YOUR PRIORITIES ARE OUT OF SYNC?

"The key is not to prioritize what's on your schedule, but to schedule your priorities." Stephen Covey once hit the nail on the head with this gem. If you're nodding along, you're like me and the hundreds of moms I've spoken with, who have, at one point or another, felt overwhelmed with a seemingly endless list of tasks.

So, how do you know if your priorities are out of sync or mixed up? Well, let's dive into that.

You know that gnawing feeling of unease that settles in your gut, or the niggling sense that something is off-balance, as you hurry through the routines of your day? That is the alarm bell your body and mind are ringing out, signaling that your priorities might be slightly, or perhaps wildly, off-kilter.

First off, you find yourself reacting, not planning. In other words, you are consistently putting out fires rather than taking preventative measures. You race from one thing to the next, always seeming to be a step behind. It feels like you're on a hamster wheel, scurrying hard but going nowhere. Your day ends in exhaustion, but the sense of accomplishment is missing.

Second, you're always busy, yet the important things still need to be done. You're swamped, no question about it. The laundry, meals, work, and kids it's a never-ending circus. But when the day comes to a close, those things that matter most, like spending quality time with your kids or engaging in self-care, are somehow pushed to the back burner yet again.

Third, you feel a constant sense of guilt. You can't shake off the guilt of not giving enough, not being there enough, not doing enough. When you're working, you're fretting about not being with your kids. And when you're with your kids, you worry about the looming deadlines. You're perpetually torn between responsibilities, feeling like you're shortchanging something or, worse, someone.

Lastly, your health and relationships may start to suffer. The energy you once had seems like a distant memory, and stress is your new shadow. Your partner feels like a roommate, and your friends... well, you can hardly remember when you last had a non-rushed, meaningful conversation.

Now, let's pause and take a deep breath. Remember, we've all been there. Recognizing these signs is the first step in reclaiming your well-deserved 'me' moments.

And the first step in our path of reclaiming our time and sanity, dear reader, is understanding where our time is currently being spent. Well, let's roll up our sleeves and dive right into it.

So, here's a simple exercise for you. Grab a paper and a pen, or open a new note on your phone. Start by listing your current responsibilities and tasks. Everything, from the monumental to the mundane, jot it down. Yes, even that five minutes you spend scrolling through social media while waiting for your coffee to brew. Remember, we're trying to capture a holistic picture here.

After listing your current responsibilities and tasks, categorize them into four quadrants based on their importance and urgency, just like the Eisenhower Matrix, if you've heard of it. The goal here is to get a clear picture of where you're spending most of your time and how much of it is spent on things that truly matter to you. It's like taking a snapshot of your day, a photo that captures the essence of your time approach.

Now, let's add a little structure to our list. The four quadrants you should have are:

Important and urgent: These tasks demand immediate attention and contribute significantly to your life. It could be things like attending your child's parent-teacher meeting or an impending work deadline.

Important but not urgent: These tasks are essential for your long-term goals or wellbeing but do not require immediate attention. This could include things like regular exercise or planning a weekend getaway with your family.

Not important but urgent: Tasks that demand your immediate attention but do not contribute significantly to your life fall into this category. An example might be answering an urgent phone call when you're in the middle of something important.

Not important and not urgent: These are tasks that neither contribute to your life nor require your immediate attention. Spending excessive time on social media might fall into this category.

Once you've categorized your tasks, step back and take a look. Where are you spending most of your time? Are you, like many of us, caught in the endless loop of urgency, neglecting what's truly important or wasting precious moments on tasks that don't serve you at all?

The goal here is not to induce guilt or regret but to provide clarity. A clear picture of our current reality is the foundation upon which we build our desired future. It's the first step towards moving from a life of constant firefighting to one of calm and control, from being a servant of time to becoming its master.

JESSICA'S WAKE-UP CALL

Now, let's get back to Jessica to see how her life story hit the turning point. A whip-smart corporate finance pro, and mom to three young kids, she is a force to be reckoned with. A hard-working, high-achieving dynamo, always on the go. A whirlwind of productivity, juggling roles like an expert circus performer.

But here's the thing about whirlwinds, they leave a trail of chaos behind them. Jessica, in all her formidable capabilities, was on a runaway train, with her eyes set only on the next task, the next deadline. The result? A trail of missed school plays, hastily cooked dinners, canceled date nights, and one very significant wake-up call.

Jessica fell seriously ill. It was life or death for a while. No one should have to go through that, but life has a way of throwing curveballs when we least expect them. And for Jessica, it was a jolt, a stark, shuddering moment of realization.

She was stretched thin, trying to conquer the corporate world while also striving to be the perfect mom, and in the process, she was missing out on the very thing she was working so hard for—her family and herself. That week spent in the sterile, quiet confines of the hospital, her kids clutching her hand, was a wake-up call, loud and clear. It echoed in the hollows of the empty boardroom meetings she wasn't attending and bounced off the walls of her now quiet home.

Jessica's example serves as a stark reminder that life is a juggling act, and as moms, we sometimes forget to keep our wellbeing in the mix. Self-care for Jessica was a concept buried under mountains of spreadsheets and laundry. She was the 'I-can-do-it-all' mom, not realizing that sometimes it's okay, necessary even, to let go and ask for help.

Jessica's wake-up call was not a gentle nudge but a gut punch. But it got her to stop and reevaluate her priorities. She realized she had to redefine her measures of success. It wasn't just about the next promotion or a sparkling clean home. It was about those precious, fleeting moments with her children. The belly laughs, the butterfly kisses, the 'I love you, mom's. It was about nurturing her relationships, her passions, and her health. It was a significant step in managing her time as a mom.

She realized that prioritizing and allocating specific blocks of time for different activities was what she desperately needed. Dedicating focused, uninterrupted time to her children and their needs, such as playing, reading, or helping with homework, became her number one priority. She realized that her constantly distracted state of mind needed to change, so she embraced distraction minimization by sending her phone on "vacation" when spending time with her family, gently bringing her attention to the present moment when work-related thoughts would start creeping in. Working from home "overtime" did not have to interrupt her family time as well, so it was planned for after the kids went to bed.

Around that priority, she set aside specific blocks of time for household chores, self-care, and other commitments. These steps helped her avoid multitasking and promoted better focus.

Remember, finding a balance that works for you may take some trial and error. Be flexible and willing to adjust your strategies as needed. By making conscious choices and focusing on what truly matters, you can manage your responsibilities effectively.

Now, I'd like you to take a moment and reflect on Jessica's story. Are there parallels in your own life? Are you juggling so much that you've forgotten to catch your wellbeing in the process? It's time to reassess. Write down your priorities, and separate the 'musts' from the 'nice-to-haves'. Remember, it's okay to say no. It's okay to delegate. It's okay to take time for yourself. Because, trust me, you are one of your family's priorities.

HOW DO WE DISCOVER OUR REAL PRIORITIES?

"Action expresses priorities," Mahatma Gandhi once said, and boy, he hit the nail right on the head, didn't he?

Now, let's talk about priorities. I'm not talking about the never-ending to-do list taped to your fridge or the calendar notifications pinging on your phone. I'm talking about the core stuff, the stuff that fuels you, makes you who you are, your values.

You see, we often confuse being busy with being productive, filling our time with tasks that don't really align with what's important to us. We do things out of obligation, habit, or the dreaded 'because I should', losing sight of what truly matters.

Take a moment to reflect - what are your values? What do you want and don't want in life? Is it family? Health? Peace of mind? Career advancement? There's no right or wrong answer here. These are your values, unique as your fingerprint.

Once you've identified your values, you've got your roadmap. Now, every decision, big or small, should line up with this roadmap. Remember, your time is precious, a non-renewable resource, and you should invest it in what matters to you.

Now, this is easier said than done. I hear you. Getting pulled into the vortex of life's non-essentials is so easy. Here's a tool that might help. It's called the "Not-to-do list". This isn't just about tasks or errands; it includes relationships, obligations, and commitments that don't add value to your life, that drain your energy rather than fuel it.

Think about it. Is there something in your life that's dragging you down? It may be a commitment that's more a burden than a joy. It's time to reassess to make some tough calls. It's time to create your "Not-to-do list" and make space for what really counts.

Speaking of which, are you giving time to everything that matters? Your health, emotional wellbeing, family, social connections, and work? It's a delicate act maintaining this balance. But it's vital. Keep a check on this. Track it because an imbalance in any area will throw off your whole game.

Believe me, there's a sublime satisfaction in aligning your life with your values and your true priorities. The chaos subsides, your time stretches, and you begin to live authentically and meaningfully. And at the end of the day, isn't that what we all want?

HOW TO PRIORITIZE DAY-TO-DAY

Remember how the old adage goes? "Eat a live frog first thing in the morning, and nothing worse will happen to you the rest of the day." - Nicolas Chamfort. No, I don't mean literally hunting down amphibians. But think about it. If you could tackle your most challenging tasks in the AM, just imagine how much smoother the rest of your day could go.

This idea goes hand in hand with the art of prioritization. Picture this - you're surrounded by a mountain of tasks, every single one seeming equally important. But here's a little secret. They aren't. Some tasks are just more critical than others, and recognizing this is a game-changer.

So how do you make sense of it all? The answer is surprisingly simple - make lists. Divide your tasks into 'more important' and 'less important' lists. But remember, the magic is in FOLLOWING these lists. They're not mere decorations for your planner but a roadmap for your day.

The routine might seem like a buzzkill, especially when life as a mom is already chock-full of predictability. But trust me, creating routines is like equipping yourself with a secret weapon. It's the rhythm that can help you dance through your day instead of stumbling. A morning routine to kick-start the day, a work routine to enhance productivity, an evening routine to wind down - the possibilities are endless. The key is consistency. Stick with it, and soon enough, it'll become second nature.

Now, I can almost hear you asking - "But life is unpredictable. What if something unexpected comes up?" Well, that's where the beauty of a flexible to-do list comes into play. Keep your to-do list alive, breathing and ready to adapt. Think of it as triaging your time - just like an ER doctor decides who to treat first based on the severity of their condition, determine which task needs your attention most at any given moment.

You've set your priorities. You've made your lists. You're following through. But then, you find yourself staring at a task and wondering, "Why am I doing this again?" That's when you reassess. Dive deep into the 'why' behind each task. Is it essential? Is it adding value to your life or your family's life? Or is it just there because it's 'always been there'? Not everything that's been done needs to continue to be done, especially if it's not serving you.

Imagine you're on a trek. You've packed your backpack meticulously, studied the map, and started off enthusiastically. But halfway up the hill, you feel your bag weighs you down. You're panting, your shoulders ache, and every step feels like a herculean task. What do you do? You stop. You reassess. You unload what's not essential to lighten your burden and continue your path with renewed vigor.

Life is not too different. The routine tasks we take on daily can sometimes pile up like a heavy backpack, making our path arduous and weary. The beauty of this scenario is that we hold the power to unload the unnecessary weight. The question here is - do we realize it?

You're diligently setting your priorities, creating your to-do lists, and following them through - kudos to you! But then, there comes a moment when you're knee-deep in a task, and you find yourself questioning, "Why am I doing this?" Trust that instinct. It's an invitation for you to pause and reassess.

Now, let's take a deep dive into the 'why' behind each task. Why is it on your list? Is it essential to your life or your family's life? Is it adding value, or is it merely there because it's 'always been there'?

Consider this example. You've been hand-washing your delicate clothes for years because that's how your mother did it. But now, with modern appliances that have gentle cycles, is this task essential? Is it the best use of your precious time? Probably not. It's a task that's been there simply because it's 'always been there'. Eliminating such tasks frees up your time for things that truly matter.

Or maybe you've been volunteering for every school event because you feel it's expected of you. However, if this is draining your energy and leaving you with no time for self-care, it's time to reassess. You could choose to volunteer selectively for events that you genuinely enjoy or those that align with your values.

The key here is to remember that not everything that's been done needs to continue to be done, especially if it's not serving you. A successful time management strategy is not just about doing things right; it's also about doing the right things.

Remember, the aim here is not to add more to our days but to invite more life into our days. And sometimes, this could mean doing less, doing differently, or even not doing at all. So, the next time you're staring at a task and wondering, "Why am I doing this?" allow yourself to pause, reassess, and possibly, let go.

A VALUES LIST TEMPLATE

"You have within you right now, everything you need to deal with whatever the world can throw at you."

— BRIAN TRACY

That's right.

You, dear Mom, are more powerful than you might think. And the first step in channeling this power? It's recognizing and understanding your values.

Values, you ask? Well, imagine a compass. A compass that directs you toward what truly matters to you, cutting through the noise of endless chores, errands, and obligations. That's what a values list does. It's a North Star, guiding your actions, decisions, and time use, ensuring they align with your authentic self. It brings you back to your core, especially when the world gets a bit too much.

Now, let's get down to the nitty-gritty of creating your own values list. Grab a cup of coffee, find a comfortable spot, and continue on this venture of self-discovery.

First off, take a moment to reflect. What matters most to you? What drives your decisions? What are the things you wouldn't compromise on? Jot these down, unfiltered. They include values like family, honesty, health, freedom, creativity, or whatever strikes a chord within you.

Next, prioritize. Not all values carry the same weight, and that's perfectly okay. Organize your list in order of importance. Remember, there's no right or wrong here. What matters is that it feels true to you.

Now, pause and take a look at your list. Are there values that closely align with each other? Can they be grouped under a broader value? This isn't about trimming down your list but about recognizing patterns and themes.

Here's the tricky part. You've got your list, but the world isn't always ideal, and sometimes, we find ourselves straying away from our values. That's why it's essential to identify potential obstacles. Write down what might pull you away from each value. Awareness is the first step in counteracting these forces.

Lastly, for each value and its corresponding obstacle, brainstorm actions to align your daily life with your values. It means setting boundaries, delegating tasks, or even saying 'no' more often. These are your action steps, your guide to leading a values-based life.

Aligning your daily life with your core values is the secret sauce to finding fulfillment and joy amidst the chaos of motherhood as well as the precious 'me-time' moments.

When life's struggles come knocking at your door, your values provide the framework to tackle them head-on. They help you prioritize, make decisions, and set boundaries. Essentially, they hold the power to transform your life from being reactive to proactive. But where do we start?

Consider your values and the obstacles that often veer you away from them. Let's brainstorm some actions to align your daily life with your values.

Let's say one of your core values is health. You're aware that maintaining your physical and mental wellbeing is crucial not just for you but also for your family. However, the obstacle standing in your way could be time - there doesn't seem to be enough hours in the day for a workout or a quiet meditation session. An action step for this might be to wake up half an hour earlier each day to squeeze in a quick workout or a mindful yoga session. You'd be amazed how this simple step could turbocharge your day with energy and positivity.

Or another value you hold dear is quality family time. However, the obstacle here could be work commitments or household chores that eat into your precious family hours. In such a case, an action step could be setting clear boundaries with your work timings or delegating chores among family members, thus freeing up time for those cherished family dinners or game nights.

Maybe personal growth is a value that's important to you. However, the obstacle could be constant interruptions and demands of your time, which leaves little room for your personal pursuits. An action step here could be saying 'no' more often to requests or commitments that do not serve your growth or wellbeing.

Remember, these action steps are your toolkit for navigating through the stormy seas of mom life. They are not one-size-fits-all, but rather, they are as unique as you are. So, be creative, be flexible, and most importantly, be honest with yourself when you design these steps.

Does this mean that everything will fall into place perfectly? Probably not. There will still be days of mayhem and melt-down. However, these action steps will help you return to your values, time and again. They will empower you to make choices that serve your wellbeing and happiness. And isn't that what we're striving for - a life of balance, satisfaction, and joy, a life that resonates with our values?

SUMMARY

You know that friend we all have who seems to juggle everything with seemingly effortless grace? Remember Jessica. Picture her: An energetic mom to three beautiful kids married to an equally hardworking corporate finance guy. With her successful corporate finance career, you'd think Jessica was nailing the elusive work-life balance.

But the reality? Jessica was hanging on by a thread, doing a balancing act bound to falter. And falter it did. Not in a spectacular, can't-ignore-this kind of way, but a silent and insidious intrusion into her life.

The wake-up call? It came in the form of a health crisis. Jessica fell seriously ill. Suddenly, her well-orchestrated, high-speed juggle was thrown off-kilter.

Jessica believed she could do it all and kept adding balls to her juggling act. But life, as it often does, threw in a curveball. Jessica was forced to reassess her priorities. She found herself confronting the reality of her choices.

She began questioning her decisions. Her children's once joyous piano recitals, dance practices, and soccer games seemed to have morphed into just more items on her never-ending to-do list. She realized she had been too caught up in her roles - as a successful corporate woman and a diligent mom - that she'd forgotten to prioritize.

Some chores could wait. But with her kids growing up, those moments couldn't be put on pause. She realized that she'd been running on a hamster wheel, not realizing that it was okay to step off occasionally.

The crisis was an eye-opener. It made Jessica reflect on what mattered most to her. It was time to reorder, to re-prioritize. She began making deliberate choices about where her time and energy went. Jessica learned she couldn't do it all, which was okay. She learned the power of saying no, letting go of expectations, and understanding her limitations.

Take a leaf out of Jessica's book. Understand that time is finite, but the demands on your time are not. You can't do everything, and that's okay.

Take a moment right now. Make a list of everything you believe is a priority in your life. Then, look at your daily routine. Do your daily actions reflect these priorities? If they don't, it's time to reassess, just like Jessica did.

Remember, life has a way of showing us what truly matters. Sometimes it's through a whisper, sometimes through a loud, reverberating wake-up call. Don't wait for that wake-up call. Start prioritizing now. After all, it's not about having time; it's about making time.

WORKSHEET

Exercises:

1. Reflect on your daily routines. How do they align or conflict with your values and goals? Write down examples that come to mind.

Notes:

_____

_____

2. Like Jessica, have you ever found your priorities out of sync? Discuss how it impacted your time management, lifestyle, workload, and stress levels.

Notes:

_____

_____

3. List your top five personal values. How do these values align with your current priorities and fit into your picture of time management?

Notes:

_____

_____

4. Consider the balance of essential aspects in your life, such as health, self-care, social connections, work, and family. Is there an area that needs more attention?

Notes:

5. Draft a not-to-do list. What tasks, relationships, or commitments can you eliminate to align your life with your values better and improve your time management?

Notes:

Practice Questions:

1. How did a lack of priorities affect Jessica's life and time management?

2. What was Jessica's wake-up call that made her reassess her priorities?

3. What strategies did Jessica employ to discover her real priorities?

_____

_____

4. How did Jessica prioritize her day-to-day tasks to align with her values?

_____

_____

5. What changes did Jessica make to prioritize her health and self-care?

_____

_____

Frequently Asked Questions:

1. How can I recognize if my priorities are out of sync?

_____

_____

2. What are some strategies to discover and align my life with my real priorities?

_____

_____

3. How can I maintain balance among the essential aspects of my life?

_____

_____

4. How can I better prioritize my day-to-day tasks?

5. How can I prioritize self-care as a busy mom?

Table:

Jessica's Prioritizing Steps	How It Helped Her	How It Can Help You
Identified personal values	Clarified her goals	Provides a guide for decision-making
Created a not-to-do list	Reduced unnecessary tasks	Helps focus on important tasks
Balanced essential aspects of life	Improved wellbeing	Fosters a balanced lifestyle
Prioritized daily tasks	Managed workload	Increases productivity
Prioritized self-care	Improved health	Enhances overall wellbeing

Key Takeaways:

1. Prioritizing is crucial to living a meaningful and fulfilled life.

Notes:

2. Identifying your personal values can guide you in making important decisions.

Notes:

_____

_____

3. Maintaining balance among important aspects of life is essential to wellbeing.

Notes:

_____

_____

4. Prioritizing day-to-day tasks can reduce workload and increase productivity.

Notes:

_____

_____

5. Self-care should be a priority, especially for busy moms.

Notes:

_____

_____

Action Steps:

1. Reflect on your values and write them down.

2. Review your routines and tasks, align them with your values, and create a not-to-do list.

3. Assess the balance in your life and identify areas that need more attention.

4. Plan your day-to-day tasks based on your priorities and keep your to-do list flexible.

5. Include self-care in your daily routine and prioritize it.

YOU'RE THE PILOT

"The bad news is time flies. The good news is you're the pilot."

— MICHAEL ALTSHULER

How many times have you had the "if only there were more hours in the day" conversation with other moms at the school gate?

I've lost count of the amount of times I've had that exact conversation, and until I got a handle on my own time management skills, often it was me who was starting it. Now, I like to quote Michael Altshuler – as much for myself as for the person I'm talking to. Whenever I'm feeling overwhelmed, I remind myself that I'm in control of my own experience.

But it took a lot of work to get here, and trust me, I know how tough it is for moms juggling family life, work life, and a busy social life. I've made it my mission to make the road a little easier for as many people as I can, and now I'd like to ask for your help as a fellow mom.

I truly believe that the strategies you're learning in this book are going to make a massive difference to your experience, and I want to get them to as many moms as I can. And you can help me without sacrificing more than a couple of minutes. All it takes is a short review.

By leaving a review of this book on Amazon, you'll show other moms that they can take control of their schedule, no matter how demanding it is – and better yet, you'll show them exactly where they can find the guidance they need to get there.

Simply by letting other readers know how this book has helped you and what they'll find inside, you'll lead them in the direction of the tools they need to transform their experience and truly make the most of their time.

Thank you so much for your support. We moms must stick together!

4

LEARNING TO DELEGATE

MEGAN'S STORY

In the immortal words of Erma Bombeck, "When your mother asks, 'Do you want a piece of advice?' it's a mere formality. It doesn't matter if you answer yes or no. You're going to get it anyway."

Megan is a formidable business entrepreneur and mother to four energetic children. This woman carried the weight of the world on her shoulders, not out of necessity but out of habit. With no partner to share the burden, Megan was an island, isolated and self-contained yet teeming with life and responsibilities that left little room for her own needs.

Megan was a perfectionist, a trait she had inherited from a lineage of strong, independent women who had carved their paths in life with relentless determination and a firm belief that a mother could, and should, do it all. This belief, though admirable, was both a boon and a bane. It allowed Megan to thrive professionally, growing her business with the tenacity of a lioness protecting her cubs. But it also caused her to hold on too tightly, to control too much, and inevitably, to let go of too little.

Every day, Megan's life was a symphony of meetings, school runs, business proposals, dinner preparations, project evaluations, bath times, and budget meetings. The notes of her existence intermingled and played in a relentless cacophony, never pausing, never resting. This music consumed her every moment, leaving no space for the gentle rhythm of self-care and self-reflection.

It's easy to see how this had repercussions on Megan and her family. Her children, energetic and full of life, often had to navigate the intricate maze of their mother's schedule to steal a few moments of undivided attention. Her business, though successful, was entirely dependent on her presence and threatened to crumble at the slightest hint of her absence. And Megan, the eye of this storm, found herself in a constant whirlwind of tasks, rarely stopping to breathe.

Take a moment and let Megan's story sink in. Are there echoes of your own life reverberating in her narrative? Do you also find yourself caught in a relentless pursuit of perfection, juggling multiple roles while trying to uphold the belief that you, as a mother, must do it all?

A stubborn, often self-imposed obstacle lies at the heart of the problem. Megan, like countless other mothers, grappled with her inability to relinquish control, to delegate tasks, to seek assistance, and to put her own needs first. This difficulty was not just rooted in the often-invisible pressures of motherhood but also in her profoundly ingrained sense of pride. She wore her pride like a badge of honor, a testament to her ability to handle everything alone. She equated asking for help with a manifestation of weakness, a blemish on her quest for perfection. This viewpoint added an unseen yet palpable burden that she shouldered, often oblivious to its detrimental impact on her health and relationships with those around her.

But it's not all doom and gloom. As we look deeper into Megan's story and those of other women like her, we will uncover practical methods and tools, not trite and simplistic but rather deeply rooted in real-life experiences. And remember, these tools are not about achieving perfection or 'doing it all.' They are about enabling you to make lasting changes that will help clear the clutter of life and time, and ultimately, reclaim those precious 'me' moments that you so deserve.

WHY MOMS TRY TO DO IT ALL

As mothers, we often find ourselves trapped in the myth of doing it all. It's a tall tale spun out of societal expectations and our own deeply ingrained beliefs about what it means to be a good mother. This myth, however, can lead us into a relentless cycle of perpetual doing, leaving us exhausted and stretched too thin.

Let's take a step back for a moment and examine why we often feel compelled to shoulder this Herculean task. Why do we feel the need to don our superhero capes and take on the world single-handedly?

The answer, as you might have guessed, is layered and complex. One reason is the way society views motherhood. There's this unspoken rule that to be a good mom, we must be all things to all people at all times. And that is a tall order.

How often have you felt pressured to present the perfect family picture? To always be there for every school event, never miss a soccer game, whip up gourmet meals, keep an immaculate house, and still excel in your career? It's a daunting list that can leave even the most energetic among us feeling winded.

Being a perfectionist doesn't help, either. If you're anything like me, you might have this constant urge to get everything just right. To do it all, flawlessly, without a hair out of place. And while this drive can be a powerful motivator, it can also send us spiraling into a world of unattainable expectations and endless to-do lists.

Perhaps the deepest layer of this issue lies in our core beliefs about what a mom should be doing. These are ideas we've absorbed over time from our upbringing, cultural influences, personal experiences, and societal norms. They can shape our thoughts and actions, sometimes in ways that put unnecessary pressure on us.

It's as if we're on a relentless hike, shouldering a backpack filled to the brim with hefty stones. Each stone is inscribed with a belief or expectation about motherhood that society, and often ourselves, have imposed.

We've all felt the weight of the "I should always be there for my kids" stone. Though borne out of love and parental responsibility, this expectation can sometimes lead us to the dangerous precipice of overparenting. We hover over our children's lives, sacrificing our own needs, hobbies, and aspirations in the process. It's like being caught in a storm of guilt and anxiety each time we take a breather for ourselves.

Then, there's the "I should keep a perfect home" stone. Who hasn't been entangled in the web of immaculate home photos on Instagram and Pinterest? They breed the seemingly innocent idea that our homes should look like something straight out of a glossy magazine. But here's a reality check - those perfectly curated homes are just snapshots, not the everyday living of real families with toys strewn about, laundry piled up, and dishes waiting in the sink.

And who can ignore the "I should excel at my job" stone? As we strive to break glass ceilings and climb corporate ladders, the pressure to perform can be intense. Amid it all, we're expected to switch seamlessly from the boardroom to the playroom, mastering the elusive art of work-life balance.

Each stone in our metaphorical backpack adds weight, burdening us with the quest for perfection in all spheres of our lives. It's as if we're expected to be superhuman, performing a high-wire act without faltering. Yet, what if we could shed some of these stones, lighten the load, and embrace a more authentic, less exhausting venture of motherhood?

Imagine setting aside the "I should always be there for my kids" stone. In its place, embrace the belief that it's okay, even beneficial, for our children to experience independence and cultivate resilience. Let's redefine our roles as mothers - not as omnipresent guardians but as supportive guides who provide our children the space to explore, make mistakes, and grow.

Similarly, could we replace the "I should keep a perfect home" stone with the idea that homes are meant to be lived in, not merely admired? That it's alright for things to be a bit messy or chaotic sometimes because that's the beauty of a home filled with life and laughter.

And finally, when it comes to the "I should excel at my job" stone, can we remind ourselves that we are more than our job titles or career achievements? That it's perfectly fine to seek professional satisfaction, but not at the cost of our well-being or peace of mind.

As we venture into this new mindset, we allow ourselves the freedom to navigate motherhood on our terms, making it a less burdensome, more joyous venture. Because at the end of the day, we're not just mothers - we're individuals with our dreams, desires, and passions. So, let's unzip that heavy backpack and start reevaluating the stones we've been carrying around. It's time we lightened our load and walked the path of motherhood with greater ease, joy, and authenticity.

WHY MOMS CAN'T AND SHOULDN'T DO IT ALL ON THEIR OWN

"Superwoman is a myth!" This is a quote from Arianna Huffington, co-founder of The Huffington Post, a woman who has a clear grasp on the pressures of juggling work, personal responsibilities, and motherhood. With this quote in mind, let's explore the topic at hand: why moms can't, and indeed shouldn't, try to do it all on their own.

Picture this. There's a towering mountain in front of you. Your task is to reach the peak, but instead of a lightweight backpack with essential climbing gear, you are saddled with a hefty bag brimming with the duties of motherhood. Each responsibility adds weight to your burden, from managing household chores to taking care of your children, to striving to excel in your career.

Sound familiar?

The overwhelming weight of these demands is the essence of mommy burnout. It's the constant feeling of being spread too thin, running from one task to another, and perpetually playing catch-up with time. This exhaustion doesn't just take a toll on your physical well-being but can lead to emotional and mental fatigue, causing stress, anxiety, and sometimes even resentment.

What's more, moms are often encouraged to tough it out, to soldier on without complaint in our culture that glorifies grit and resilience. But the truth is, such a culture doesn't help us;

instead, it masks the underlying problem, leading us further into the burnout cycle.

Now, let's challenge this norm. Because believe it or not, asking for help, delegating tasks, and prioritizing self-care aren't signs of weakness or failure. On the contrary, they are indicators of strength, wisdom, and self-awareness.

How so, you might ask? Well, let's put it this way - juggling everything alone isn't sustainable in the long run. Yes, you might pull it off for a while, but eventually, something's got to give. And more often than not, it's your well-being that takes the hit.

MEGAN'S BURNOUT LESSONS

"You can't pour from an empty cup." A simple yet profound quote that we've all heard, but its true essence becomes apparent only when you find yourself in a situation where your cup is dry, your reservoir is depleted, and you have nothing left to give. This brings us to the story of Megan, a tale that many moms might find all too familiar.

Megan was a supermom in every sense of the word. She was an attentive mother and an ambitious professional running a successful business. Like a tightrope walker, she always balanced, striving to harmonize her work and personal life.

However, the continuous juggling act took a toll on her over time. Her energy was dwindling, her enthusiasm was fading, and she was frequently irritable. She felt drained, and despite managing to keep the plates spinning, she was running on empty.

One evening, Megan sat at her dining table, surrounded by stacks of work files, with her kids tugging at her sleeve, asking her to play with them. She was at her wit's end. She felt torn between her responsibilities. At that moment, it hit her - she was burned out. The relentless pursuit of doing it all had left her exhausted and unhappy.

So, what did she do?

Megan realized she needed to turn things around. She needed to stop being the 'perfect' mom; and become a 'happy' mom, a 'content' mom, and an 'engaged' mom.

Her venture began with acknowledging to herself and others that she was not superhuman and could not handle everything alone. As a single mom, Megan started distributing tasks within her family and professional circles. With no partner to share her burdens, she turned to her parents and extended family for assistance. Initially, Megan hesitated to ask her elderly parents to babysit her children, doubting their ability to manage. Yet, she eventually let go of her concerns and entrusted her children to their care. To her surprise, the arrangement worked remarkably well. Not only did this delegation free up time for Megan, but it also made her parents extremely happy as they relished spending more quality time with their grandchildren. In her business, too, she reshaped her boundaries, learning to decline when the load became too heavy assertively.

Secondly, she started carving out time for self-care. It began with simple things like ensuring she ate proper meals and slept well. Then, she started scheduling 'me' time into her week. This included things she enjoyed, like reading a book, practicing yoga, or even just spending quiet moments with a cup of coffee.

Finally, Megan mastered the art of releasing her guilt. She realized that carving out personal time didn't render her an unfit mother. On the contrary, it enhanced her motherhood by allowing her to approach her kids with rejuvenated vigor and a cheerier outlook. As her children matured, Megan began assigning them some household chores. By relinquishing her quest for perfection, she enabled her kids to attempt tasks independently and learn, despite the outcome not being flawless. This not only eased her load but also created a learning opportunity for her children.

The transformation didn't happen overnight. It was a slow, continuous process with plenty of bumps along the way. But Megan persevered because she knew the alternative was a path to burnout.

Today, Megan's life might not look picture-perfect, but it feels right for her. She has found a balance that suits her needs and those of her family. She has learned to prioritize and manage her time effectively, not to do more but to live more.

Megan's story serves as a powerful reminder to all of us. As moms, it's okay not to do everything. It's okay to seek help. It's okay to put ourselves on the priority list. Remember, a happier mom means a happier family.

Let's take this as a moment of introspection. Is your cup running dry? Are you feeling the early signs of burnout? If so, it's time to reconsider your priorities and make some changes. Because, as moms, we deserve to take care of ourselves just as much as we take care of everyone else.

These tools will not only help you grasp the concepts better but also provide you with real-world examples to model your life after.

Let's start by understanding the most common problems we face:

Time Constraints: From managing household chores to our careers, time seems to slip away, leaving us with a sense of dissatisfaction and the longing for 'me' time.

Neglect of Self-Care: In the process of taking care of everyone else, we often overlook our own needs, which could lead to physical and emotional exhaustion.

Work-Family Balance: Striking a balance between professional commitments and family time is a common struggle that leaves us torn between the two.

Limited Support System: Not having a reliable support system increases our responsibilities and adds to our stress.

Constant Decision-Making: The constant need to make decisions, big and small, for the family often leads to decision fatigue, leaving us feeling drained.

Perfectionism: having rigid and unattainable standards can lead to chronic stress, anxiety, and a constant feeling of never being "good enough."

HOW CAN WE EASE OUR LOADS?

I love this quote by Anne Lamott: "Almost everything will work again if you unplug it for a few minutes, including you." It's the unvarnished truth. We all need a breather, especially us moms who sometimes feel like we're juggling flaming swords while walking on a tightrope.

So, how can we ease our loads? How can we create some breathing room in our lives?

Let's start with simplifying. Simplification is more than just decluttering your physical space. It's about trimming the fat from your life, cutting down on the commitments that don't bring joy or value. Remember, it's not just about being busy; it's about being productive. Pare down your to-do list to essentials, focusing on what matters most to you and your family. Try it out. You might find it liberating. Simplicity over perfectionism.

Next, embrace the power of the four Ds: Delete, Delegate, Defer, and Do. Consider each task on your to-do list and decide whether it's something you need to do, something that can be given to someone else (even if the outcome may be slightly imperfect for your perfectionistic mind), something that can be delayed, or something that can be deleted altogether. The aim here is to ensure that your time and energy are being used in the most effective way possible.

The third point is about self-care. I can't stress enough how crucial this is. We often confuse self-care with indulgence or being selfish. But it's not about luxury spa days or expensive retreats. It's about basic things like ensuring you're eating nutritious meals, getting enough sleep, taking breaks, and making time for things you enjoy. Taking care of yourself is not a luxury; it's a necessity.

Fourth, don't hesitate to ask for help. Many of us have a hard time with this, don't we? We think we should be able to handle everything ourselves. But remember, it's not a sign of weakness. It's a sign of being human. If you need help, ask. It could be your partner, a family member, a friend, or even a professional service. You're not in this alone.

Finally, get the kids involved. Believe it or not, kids are capable of more than we sometimes give them credit for. Assign age-appropriate tasks to your children. Not only does it take a load off you, but it also teaches them responsibility. It could be something as simple as picking up toys for the little ones or helping with meal prep for the older kids. Encourage them to take ownership of their chores. This way, they learn valuable skills while contributing to the family.

So, here's a small exercise for you. Pick one of these points that resonates most with you, and implement it for a week. Note down how it makes you feel and what changes it brings to your daily routine. The idea is to find a strategy that works best for you.

To be a mom is to live in the whirlwind, juggle, and hustle. And it's no secret that the perpetual race against time can leave us moms gasping for breath.

Let's pause for a second here. You see, motherhood, though chaotic and unpredictable, doesn't have to be an all-consuming entity that swallows your time whole. No, it's not about squeezing more hours into a day; instead, it's about making those hours work for you. And that's what we're here to unravel.

Remember when we used to juggle oranges for fun back in the day? Well, now we're juggling responsibilities - our children, home, career, social commitments, and the list goes on. And boy, these responsibilities sure don't bounce back when dropped, unlike the oranges. But what if I told you there's a way to keep those balls in the air without sacrificing your well-being?

While we're here, let's address the elephant in the room - the pain points that nibble away at your time, energy, and sanity. Balancing work and family life, tending to your self-care, dealing with constant decision-making, managing time constraints, and often facing a limited support system. Phew! That's a tall order. But that's what makes you super.

Yet, even supermoms need a breather. Trust me, your 'me' moments matter—your self-care matters. Your dreams and passions, they matter. And it's high time you reclaim them.

Think about it. How would it feel to rise above the daily hustle, to replace the frantic rush with a calm flow? To have not just the time but the energy to devote to yourself and your family? Sounds dreamy, right? But it's not a dream. It's a reality that's within your grasp.

FAMILY CHORE CHARTS

There's this saying I've come across, "You can do anything but not everything." It hit me, that's precisely it! We, moms, have this superhuman drive to do it all, don't we? But let's be honest, our day only has 24 hours, and that's a fact we can't change. What we can change, however, is how we use those hours.

Let's explore a couple of tools that can help us navigate our days more efficiently. Think of it as remodeling your toolbox for life management. These tools are a family chore chart and a surprising yet effective not-to-do list.

First, let's chat about family chore charts. If you're imagining a colorful poster with gold stars and happy faces stickers, that's one way to do it, especially if you've got younger kids. However, a chore chart can be a detailed list as well. The magic happens when you assign tasks to each family member, making everyone accountable for their part in maintaining the household. It's a great way to lighten your load and teach your kids responsibility.

You can create a simple chart or get a bit creative with it. There are plenty of ideas online if you need some inspiration, but the point is to make it work for your family. Tailor it to your needs. Assign age-appropriate tasks, set clear expectations, and throw in some rewards for an added incentive. Give it a try; you might be surprised by how much help you get around the house.

Here are a few examples of how you might structure your own family chore chart:

Basic Family Chore Chart: This is the most straightforward format. Divide a chart into rows and columns. Each row represents a family member, and each column represents a day of the week. Write each person's chores in their corresponding row and column.

Rotating Chore Chart: This chart is helpful for families where chores are switched on a weekly or monthly basis. The structure is similar to the basic chart, but the assignments move between family members based on the rotation schedule.

Age-Appropriate Chore Chart: This chart is divided by age groups (toddlers, school-age children, teens) with chores that are suitable for each age group. For example, toddlers can pick up toys, school-age children can make their beds, and teens can wash dishes.

Reward-Based Chore Chart: This chart not only assigns chores but also assigns rewards for completed chores. Rewards could be some extra time of video games, a special dessert, or anything that motivates your children.

Color-Coded Chore Chart: This visually appealing chart uses different colors for each family member. Assign a color to each person and use their color to write their chores. This method makes it easy to see at a glance who is responsible for what.

Magnetic Chore Chart: This chart uses magnets that are moved around to assign and track chores. You can write chores on individual magnets and move them from a "to-do" area to a "done" area.

Digital Chore Chart: There are many apps and online tools available now that allow you to create and manage a chore chart digitally. These can often include features like reminders, checklists, and reward trackers.

NOT-TO-DO LISTS

There's a somewhat offbeat path that only a few talk about in the realm of time management. You are very well familiar with various to-do lists scribbled on notepads or neatly organized in fancy apps, brimming with tasks we need to conquer. We hold it close, almost like a sacred treasure map leading us to the land of productivity. But have you ever thought of having a "Not-to-do list"? A list of tasks, habits, or commitments you intentionally choose to avoid to make room for what truly matters?

You might be surprised at how this slightly radical concept can work wonders. Picture an overburdened mom juggling her kids, work, chores, and perhaps a part-time study. She's like a circus performer spinning multiple plates at once; understandably, it's exhausting. She has a list of chores, tasks, errands, stretching as long as a country road. But now, she's got herself a not-to-do list. This list is her ticket to reclaiming precious hours. It holds tasks she's decided to cut down, delegate, or eliminate entirely. It's her way of saying, 'These are tasks I need not burden myself with.'

It's a pretty liberating thought, isn't it? A not-to-do list doesn't necessarily mean you're neglecting your responsibilities. On the contrary, it's about setting priorities straight. It's about understanding that you can't, and shouldn't, try to do it all. By identifying tasks and activities that aren't serving your goals, you're paving the way for enhanced productivity and reduced stress. Now, how wonderful is that?

Let's make this tangible with a practical exercise. Grab a sheet of paper and draw two columns. Label one as "To-do" and the other as "Not-to-do". Under the "To-do" list, write down tasks that align with your priorities and contribute to your objectives. These are your non-negotiables. Next, fill the "Not-to-do" column with tasks that take up significant time but contribute little to your goals. Remember to include habits that drain your energy and create unnecessary clutter in your life.

Remember, this isn't about creating an exhaustive list. Instead, consider it a fluid, evolving tool that adapts to your ever-changing life circumstances. Some days your not-to-do list may include skipping the news or avoiding non-urgent emails. On other days, it might be about stepping away from social media or saying 'no' to tasks you can delegate.

This one is a bit counter-intuitive, but stick with me. Often, we are so focused on what we need to do that we overlook the things we should stop doing. These are the time-drainers, the unnecessary tasks, the commitments we've taken on just because we didn't know how to say 'no.'

This tool helps you identify and eliminate the non-essentials in your life. Start by listing things that take up your time without adding value to your life or aligning with your priorities. It could be something as simple as spending too much time on social media or constantly checking your emails. Once you've identified these culprits, make a conscious decision to stop or at least reduce these activities. Remember, every 'no' to a non-essential means a 'yes' to something that truly matters to you.

Here's a little challenge for you. Make a family chore chart and a not-to-do list for the upcoming week. Remember, they don't have to be fancy or elaborate. They need to be functional and suitable for your family. Try them out and observe the changes. Take notes if that's your thing. See what works, what doesn't, and adjust as needed. You might just discover a new way to make your day run a little smoother.

SUMMARY

Megan was, and still is, one of the most inspiring people I've ever met. She's a business entrepreneur, juggling the dizzying demands of her own business with raising four wonderfully energetic kids. Megan's a fighter, a force to be reckoned with, but as the days turned into months and the months into years, her fire began to flicker.

You see, Megan had a tendency to cling to everything, from managing the house to sorting out her kids' lunches, from overseeing her business operations to scheduling and attending countless meetings. If a task was on the horizon, Megan wanted to handle it personally.

She thought she could do it all, and for a while, she did. Megan was a whirlwind, zipping from one task to another, from one role to another: a mother, an entrepreneur, and a friend. And to anyone looking in from the outside, she seemed to have it all under control. But behind her beaming smile and sparkling eyes, Megan was struggling. The burden of trying to handle it all was taking its toll on her.

That's the tricky thing about trying to handle it all by yourself. At first, it feels like empowerment, like you're conquering the world. But over time, it turns into an unbearable weight. Like you're Atlas, carrying the world on your shoulders, with no end in sight.

Megan's story is a stark reminder that letting go is okay. Letting go doesn't mean you're giving up or shirking your responsibilities. It simply means you're acknowledging your limits. You understand you're human, and asking for help is okay. It's okay to delegate, lean on others and share the load.

So, let's learn from Megan's journey. Take a moment to reflect on your own life. What are the things you're holding onto simply because you're afraid to let go? What are the tasks you can delegate or share? And most importantly, how can you start taking better care of yourself so you don't end up burned out and overwhelmed like Megan?

Remember, letting go isn't a sign of weakness. It's a sign of strength. It shows you value yourself, and you understand the importance of balance. After all, you can't pour from an empty cup. Take care of yourself first, and everything else will fall into place.

WORKSHEET

Exercises:

1. Reflect on your current responsibilities. Are there tasks you're holding onto that could be delegated or let go? Write down examples.

Notes:

_____

_____

2. Like Megan, have you ever found yourself trying to do it all? Discuss its impact on your time management, lifestyle, workload, and stress levels.

Notes:

_____

_____

3. Write down any beliefs you hold about what a mom should be doing. Where do these beliefs come from, and how are they influencing your actions?

Notes:

_____

_____

4. Have you ever experienced burnout due to trying to do it all? Reflect on this experience and the steps you took to recover.

Notes:

_____

_____

5. Consider ways to simplify your life. Draft a not-to-do list and identify tasks you can delegate or defer.

Notes:

_____

_____

Practice Questions:

1. What beliefs did Megan hold that contributed to her trying to do it all?

_____

_____

2. How did Megan's inability to let go impact her and her family?

_____

_____

3. What was the turning point for Megan in her journey towards delegating and letting go?

_____

_____

4. What strategies did Megan use to ease her load and prevent burnout?

5. How did Megan involve her kids in taking responsibility and easing the household load?

Frequently Asked Questions:

1. Why do some moms feel they must do it all?

2. What are some signs of burnout due to trying to do it all?

3. How can I simplify my life and prevent burnout?

4. How can I delegate tasks effectively?

5. How can I involve my kids in household responsibilities?

_____

_____

Table:

Megan's Burnout Prevention Steps	How It Helped Her	How It Can Help You
Simplified her life	Reduced stress	Promotes peace and balance
Practiced real self-care	Improved health	Enhances overall wellbeing
Delegated tasks	Managed workload	Increases free time and productivity

Key Takeaways:

1. Moms can't and shouldn't do it all on their own. It's a path to burnout.

Notes:

_____

_____

2. Letting go of perfectionism and delegating tasks can ease the load and prevent burnout.

Notes:

_____

_____

3. Asking for help is crucial, not a sign of weakness.

Notes:

4. Involving kids in household responsibilities can ease the load and teach them responsibility.

Notes:

5. Real self-care and simplifying life are powerful ways to manage stress and prevent burnout.

Notes:

Action Steps:

1. Identify tasks you can delegate or defer, and make a not-to-do list.

2. Implement real self-care practices in your daily routine.

3. Ask for help when you need it, either from your family or your community.

4. Involve your kids in household responsibilities according to their age and abilities.

5. Continually reassess your workload and stress levels to prevent burnout.

MAGIC OF SAYING "NO"

LAUREN'S STORY

Stephanie Lahart once wrote, "Let today mark a new beginning for you. Give yourself permission to say NO without feeling guilty, mean, or selfish. Anybody who gets upset or expects you to say yes all of the time clearly doesn't have your best interest at heart. Always remember: You have a right to say no without having to explain yourself. Be at peace with your decisions."

Meet Lauren, an emblem of strength and perseverance but also a reflection of countless mothers who, like her, struggle with an inability to say 'no'. She's a warm-hearted, generous woman, a mom of two, and together with her loving husband, they have adopted another child out of the goodness of their hearts. Her household is currently bustling with her immediate family and her husband's extended family. Yes, that's right - imagine that setting. It's a colorful panorama of shared meals, boisterous laughter, and memories in the making, a large family home bustling with activity from dawn till dusk. The kids are off to school and the elders need care; there are meals to prepare, a house to clean, homework to supervise, and a job to keep. Lauren is exceptionally proud of her big loud family, yet, at the same time, all these responsibilities rest heavily on Lauren's shoulders.

The setting has become a whirlpool of tasks, responsibilities, and expectations where she was perpetually caught. Her generosity and cultural obligation have led to her current situation – overwhelmingly snowed under with a plethora of tasks and expectations.

Lauren hails from a culturally rich, diverse background that instills the value of service and sacrifice. She's been brought up with the idea that a good wife, mother, and daughter-in-law always puts the needs of her family before her own. So, she finds it hard to say 'no' when asked for help or when a new task lands on her already overcrowded plate.

For instance, when relatives come to visit unannounced, she spends hours preparing food and making up rooms for them. When her kids volunteer her for school activities, she is always there, whether it's baking for a charity sale or chaperoning a school trip. Her own needs, her 'me-time', have become an elusive dream, perpetually pushed back to accommodate the needs of others. Saying 'no' was not an option. It was as if the word had been wiped from her dictionary, replaced instead by "yes, sure," "I can do that," and "Don't worry." But, often, the beauty of these values is tainted by the weight of expectations they entail, especially for women who are always ready to serve others, like Lauren. The paradox was that while everyone around her relied on her ability to manage things, no one seemed to have the time or inclination to lend her a helping hand. Overwhelmed is an understatement for her condition.

This cycle of endlessly giving, of not being able to refuse, is taking its toll on her. She is frequently exhausted, her health has taken a backseat, and she barely has time to breathe, let alone indulge in hobbies or relaxation.

Let's look deeper into a few instances that will give you a glimpse into Lauren's struggles.

One day, she was juggling meal preparation and helping her kids with homework while also trying to meet a deadline for her work-from-home job. Seeing her already swamped with tasks, her sister-in-law came up to her with yet another request, "Lauren, can you please look after my kids too? I have an important event to attend." Lauren's mind screamed a resounding 'no,' but the word that slipped out was an obliging 'yes.'

On another occasion, her husband asked her to accompany him to a late-night friend's get-together after a long day. Lauren yearned for a peaceful night's sleep. But, worried about disappointing her husband, she suppressed her fatigue, managed a smile, and agreed.

The reluctance to say 'no' was slowly but surely, snatching away Lauren's happiness and peace. It was corroding her relationship with her family as resentment started to creep in. Worse still, it was making her lose sight of herself.

But as they say, the darkest hour is just before the dawn. Lauren's moment of clarity arrived, and it started with her recognizing that the power to change her circumstances lay within her. That change was the simple, two-letter word – "No."

Now, this is where we start focusing on the light at the end of the tunnel and cultivating assertiveness: Saying 'no' does not equate to rudeness. It is about respecting your limits. Practicing phrases like "I cannot take this on right now" or "Can we find another solution?" can tremendously affect your life.

WHY WE DON'T LIKE TO SAY 'NO'

Remember Claudia Black's words: "Saying no can be the ultimate self-care." Let's explore why saying 'no' feels like the forbidden fruit in a world that celebrates relentless yeses.

As we reflect on Lauren's tale, we might wonder why it is so hard to say 'no' for many of us, even when we're sinking in the sea of expectations, responsibilities, and tasks. We know we need to say it, and we understand the importance, but the word just doesn't come out. The reason behind this struggle is as complex and multifaceted as we are. So, let's pull up a chair, maybe grab a cup of your favorite brew, and unravel the mystery behind our often-debilitating inability to say 'no.'

Firstly, many of us worry about disappointing others. Think about the last time you said 'yes' when you desperately wanted to say 'no.' Was it because you didn't want to let someone down? Perhaps it was your boss who piled on another project when you were already working overtime or a friend who needed a last-minute babysitter for their toddler on the night you planned to unwind. We tend to overcommit because we don't want to disappoint others. Yet, in the process, we disappoint the most critical person - ourselves.

Here's an illustrative example - imagine being a pastry chef. Your friend asks you to bake a five-tier wedding cake, knowing well that you're swamped with orders. You're hesitant but agree because you want to please them. Consequently, you work longer hours, sacrificing your downtime, and your other orders suffer. You please your friend but at what cost?

Secondly, our fear of conflict can make us reluctant to say 'no.' We worry that our 'no' might upset the other person, instigate an argument, or even strain the relationship. So, we find it easier to agree than to create potential friction. It's almost like being a surfer who chooses to ride the wave, no matter how massive, instead of facing the risk of being toppled by it.

For instance, consider you are part of a neighborhood committee planning a block party. The team wants to host an extravagant event, but you prefer a low-key affair for budgetary reasons. However, fearing disagreement or a heated discussion, you go with the majority. As a result, you have to shell out more money and deal with unnecessary stress.

Thirdly, societal and cultural conditioning often fuels our difficulty in saying 'no.' We are taught to be accommodating, helpful, and selfless, especially women. Refusal is often associated with being rude, selfish, or unkind, which deters us from asserting our boundaries.

Imagine growing up in a family where you're taught that children should always comply with adults' requests without any refusal. As you grow older, this belief may carry forward, making it challenging for you to say 'no' to authority figures, despite your discomfort or the impact on your well-being.

Finally, there's the desire to be liked and accepted. We often say 'yes' because we want to be reliable, helpful, or kind. We fear that saying 'no' might tarnish our image and make us less likable.

Let's take the example of a workplace setting. You're already working late hours, but when your colleague asks you to help with their project, you agree, hoping to be seen as a team player. You don't want to be perceived as non-cooperative or selfish. However, the additional work takes a toll on your health and personal life.

Recognizing why we find it hard to say 'no' is the first step toward addressing this issue. By understanding the underlying reasons, we can consciously work towards setting boundaries, preserving our time and energy, and ultimately, enhancing our life's quality.

DO YOU LACK BOUNDARIES?

Isn't it fascinating how we dive deeper into these currents of time management and come face-to-face with an underlying treasure – the concept of boundaries? The journey from saying 'no' inevitably leads us to this vital station. So, let's take a moment to understand this concept and its intricate weave in the tapestry of our lives.

We all have our unique comfort zones. That personal bubble where we feel safe, respected, and in control. That is the boundary – your emotional, physical, and mental limit defining what's acceptable to you and what's not. But here's a question - are your boundaries well-defined, or are they so blurry that anyone can trespass them anytime?

Imagine a beautiful garden brimming with vibrant flowers, lush trees, and perhaps a little pond with ducks. Now, picture this garden without a fence. Anyone can enter, trample the flowers, disturb the serenity, and you're left cleaning the mess. On the other hand, a garden with a fence is still welcoming, but it ensures that your beautiful space is respected and protected. That's precisely what healthy boundaries do.

Healthy boundaries are like the fence around your garden. They protect your mental and emotional space, preserving your energy for things that matter most to you. They ensure respect for your time, your feelings, your needs, and your personal space. They enable you to separate your thoughts and feelings from those of others, safeguarding your autonomy.

Let's take an example here. Suppose you have a friend who often unloads their problems on you, leaving you drained emotionally. Setting a healthy boundary here might look like letting your friend know that while you care about their issues, you also need to protect your emotional well-being and can't always be available for these intense conversations.

In contrast, unhealthy boundaries are like a broken or non-existent fence around your garden. They allow others to invade your space, dictate your decisions, and deplete your energy. They make you feel responsible for others' happiness and well-being, leaving you feeling guilty if you prioritize your needs.

For instance, if you have a colleague who always leaves their part of a team project for the last minute and expects you to cover for them, that's a classic case of unhealthy boundaries. If you're unable to stand up for yourself and end up sacrificing your personal time to complete their work, it's a sign that you need to redefine your boundaries.

WHY DO WE NEED TO SET BOUNDARIES AND LEARN TO SAY 'NO'?

If you ever feel guilty about setting boundaries, remember what Brene Brown said: "Daring to set boundaries is about having the courage to love ourselves, even when we risk disappointing others." We'll look into why setting boundaries and learning to say 'no' is crucial.

Ah, it's incredible, isn't it? How all these pieces of the puzzle - the struggle to say 'no' and the blurry boundaries - all link together in this intricate matrix that forms our life. But now that we've explored the concept of boundaries let's dive into why they are so darn important and why we must muster the courage to utter that simple yet powerful word – 'no'.

Let's think about our lives as a movie, and you, are the director of your own blockbuster. Now, imagine a movie set with no rules, schedules, or clear roles. What would happen? Chaos! That's what our lives could be like without boundaries – a chaotic mess where it's hard to distinguish your needs from those of others, where your energy gets sapped before you can use it for the things you love. Boundaries, in essence, are the unseen guidelines that help to keep our life's movies on track.

We must set boundaries primarily for one reason - to protect and take care of ourselves. They serve as a 'do not disturb' sign that signals respect for our personal space and time. They give us permission to put ourselves first, not out of selfishness, but to ensure we can give our best to those we care about. Setting boundaries also builds self-esteem and reduces stress, anxiety, and feelings of resentment.

Consider a scenario where you've agreed to help with a community event. The initial ask was for a couple of hours each week, but as the event draws near, those few hours have expanded to take up entire weekends. Your family time suffers, and you're feeling overwhelmed. Here, setting a boundary means having a frank conversation about your time commitment, expressing that while you're happy to help, your availability isn't limitless.

And that brings us to saying 'no'. Why is it important to be able to say 'no'? In essence, every time you say 'yes' when you want to say 'no', you're handing over control of your time and energy to someone else. It's like you're signing off on a blank check, and we all know where that leads. Saying 'no' allows you to retain that control, ensuring that your time and energy are spent on the things that truly matter to you.

LAUREN'S TURNING POINT

In this section, we'll explore Lauren's 'aha' moment, her turning point that redefined the boundaries of her life.

We've unraveled quite a bit of our mystery and seen the dots connecting, lines intersecting. Now let's return to Lauren's tale and discover the moment that changed everything, the catalyst in her journey.

In all its unpredictability, life has a peculiar way of slapping us awake at times. You trudge along the beaten path, one step after another, until suddenly, a turning point appears that thrusts you off course. These pivotal moments, often arriving in the cloak of crisis or epiphany, grab you by the collar and shake you out of the monotony. Lauren, too, had such an earth-shattering moment.

It was during the thick of wedding season, a particularly stressful time in Lauren's household. Picture this: Lauren was juggling her work, managing her children's routine, playing host to the extended family who had taken up residence in her home, and fulfilling the endless list of responsibilities that come with having a big family. A parade of rituals, shopping sprees, socializing - there was no end. But even in this frenzy, she was expected to hold it all together, the sturdy pillar that wouldn't crumble.

One night, after a long day of festivities, Lauren was alone in the kitchen, clearing up the remnants of the day's celebrations. Her eyes were drawn to the reflection in the window - a worn-out woman in her late thirties, fatigued yet unable to rest, with an undercurrent of desperation visible in her eyes. And at that moment, it hit her. It felt like she was seeing herself clearly for the first time. She realized she had become a passenger in her own life, a marionette dancing to the tune of others' expectations. It was a chilling revelation, a stark confrontation with a reality she had ignored for too long.

This epiphany was her awakening. Lauren realized that she had been so caught up in fulfilling the roles of a mother, wife and daughter-in-law that she had lost her sense of self. She was a 'yes woman,' never challenging, always accommodating. She had built a fortress of 'yes' around herself, a fortress that was suffocating her.

Lauren, who had juggled roles, responsibilities, and expectations with as much grace as she could muster, was suddenly acutely aware of the imbalance in her life. She recognized her inability to say 'no,' her lack of boundaries, and the toll it was taking on her physical and mental wellbeing. She realized that she was not just a cog in the wheel of her family but an individual who had dreams, desires, and the right to her own time and space.

It was a turning point, a moment of self-realization that spurred Lauren toward change. This moment, painful as it was, kindled a spark within her - a determination to reclaim control over her life, to give voice to her needs and wants, to redraw her boundaries, and most importantly, to learn the power of saying 'no.'

PUTTING BOUNDARIES IN PLACE RESPECTFULLY

As we venture forward, let's unravel how you can respect your own boundaries while honoring others'.

Setting respectful boundaries, saying 'no' without fear, and freeing ourselves from the shackles of guilt might sound challenging, but trust me, with a bit of practice, you'll notice a significant enhancement in your personal and professional relationships. So, buckle up, and let's dive right in!

1. Establishing Respectful Boundaries

Setting boundaries isn't about putting walls between you and others. Instead, it's about creating a respectful and considerate space where everyone's needs and preferences are valued. Here's how you can do it:

- *Communicate Openly*: Honesty is the bedrock of any relationship. Start by openly communicating your needs, discomforts, or reservations about any situation. For instance, let's consider you're consistently being asked to work overtime, and it's impacting your personal life. Instead of suffering in silence, express your concern to your manager, illustrating your dilemma with real-life examples of how it's affecting you.
- *Assertiveness is Key*: Assertiveness isn't about being aggressive; it's about confidently expressing your needs and desires. Consider a situation where a friend consistently borrows money and fails to return it.

Instead of tolerating it, you can assertively say, "I value our friendship and want to help, but I also need to manage my finances responsibly. Therefore, I can't lend any more money until the previous debts are cleared."

2. Saying 'No' for the First Time

If you've been conditioned to be a people-pleaser, saying 'no' might seem intimidating. But don't worry; you can get there:

- *Prepare and Practice*: The first 'no' is always the hardest. Practice with low-stakes situations. If you usually take on extra tasks at work, try saying, "I'm currently swamped with this project. Maybe someone else can assist?" By doing so, you're not just saying 'no', but also providing a solution.
- *Keep It Simple and Firm*: There's no need for elaborate explanations. A simple "I won't be able to make it" or "I can't commit to this right now" is sufficient. Once, when asked to join a community event during a busy week, a simple, "I appreciate the invitation, but I won't be able to participate due to prior commitments" will suffice. Firmness in tone can prevent further persuasion attempts.

3. Letting Go of Guilt

Guilt can be a heavy burden to bear, but remember, it's okay to prioritize your needs:

- *Understand Your Worth*: Acknowledge that your needs, feelings, and desires are just as valid as others'. Prioritizing your mental health over an optional social event is perfectly okay. If a friend invites you to a party, but you're feeling drained, it's okay to say, "I really need a quiet night in. Let's catch up another time." No guilt attached!
- *Self-Compassion is Crucial*: Remember, you're not selfish for saying 'no' or setting boundaries. Practice self-compassion, understanding that it's okay not to please everyone on the regular basis. Reflecting on times when you successfully prioritized your needs over guilt-inducing requests can bolster your confidence.

WHAT YOU CAN DO IF PEOPLE DON'T RESPECT YOUR 'NO' OR YOUR BOUNDARIES

Now that we've learned about setting boundaries, saying 'no', and releasing guilt, let's explore what happens when people don't respect your boundaries. After all, change isn't always welcomed by everyone around us. But don't worry! We've got you covered with some tried and tested strategies to manage such situations effectively. Let's roll!

1. Managing Boundary Violations

Even after setting clear boundaries, you might find people who struggle to respect them. This can be a difficult situation, but there are effective ways to handle it:

- *Be Consistent and Assertive*: Maintain your stance firmly but kindly. For instance, if a colleague continues to dump their workload onto you, reassert your boundary by saying, "I understand that you're swamped, but I've got my own tasks to handle as well. Maybe we can talk to our manager and find a solution?"
- *Don't Be Afraid to Escalate*: If someone continues to disregard your boundaries, don't hesitate to escalate the matter to a person of authority, if applicable. For example, if you're facing continued boundary violations at work, speak to your supervisor or HR about the situation. You're not creating trouble; you're merely advocating for your rights.

2. Responding to Disrespect of Your 'No'

Saying 'no' is a right, not a privilege. If someone doesn't respect your refusal, here's what you can do:

- *Stay Calm and Collected*: Keep your emotions in check. Becoming angry or upset can escalate the situation. Suppose a friend repeatedly pressures you to attend late-night parties despite your refusal. You might say, "I understand these events are fun for you, but they're not my scene. I value our friendship and hope you can respect my preferences as I respect yours."

- *Reiterate and Explain*: Sometimes, people need to understand the 'why' behind your 'no'. Clarify your reasons without feeling guilty or defensive. When a family member keeps asking for financial aid despite your refusal, you might explain, "I'm currently focusing on building my savings, and I can't provide financial help as frequently as before. I'm more than happy to help you figure out a budget or find other resources, though."

Remember, maintaining boundaries and asserting your 'no' might not be a smooth sail. There may be waves that try to topple your boat. But with calmness, consistency, and assertiveness, you can navigate these waters successfully. Not everyone will respect your journey, but it's important to remember that this journey is yours, not theirs.

Now, let's engage in a hands-on activity where you can look deeper into your likes, dislikes, and personal boundaries. You're in the driver's seat of this exploration, and I'm here to guide you. So, let's dive in!

1. The Self-Reflection Exercise

This exercise involves introspection and self-awareness. Here's how to do it:

- *Identify Your Likes and Dislikes*: Begin by listing out your likes and dislikes in different areas of your life. This could include work, relationships, leisure, and even self-care. For instance, you might enjoy working in a team but dislike being burdened with extra tasks. Perhaps you love spending time with friends but dislike late-night parties. Be honest and comprehensive in this list.

- *Highlight Your Boundaries*: Reflect on your dislikes list and identify which of these dislikes stem from your boundaries being crossed. For instance, being loaded with extra tasks could violate your work-life balance. Late-night parties might be infringing on your need for restful sleep.

2. The Boundary-Setting Exercise

Having identified potential areas where your boundaries are being crossed, let's learn to articulate them clearly:

- *Define Your Boundaries*: For each identified boundary, articulate what a respectful acknowledgment of that boundary looks like. For instance, a respectful boundary for work might be: "I am dedicated to my job, but I need to maintain a healthy work-life balance. Therefore, I can't consistently work beyond regular hours."
- *Practice Expressing Your Boundaries*: Once you've defined your boundaries, the next step is to practice expressing them. Use a respectful but firm tone. Remember, these are your boundaries, and you have every right to assert

them. Rehearse these boundary statements aloud or write them down.

As you engage in this boundary-setting exercise, remember that it's okay if it feels uncomfortable or difficult initially. It's all part of the process. You're building a muscle of assertiveness and self-respect; like any muscle, it takes regular exercise to strengthen.

So, how do you feel after this exercise? Did you discover something new about your likes, dislikes, and boundaries? As we continue this voyage of self-discovery and empowerment, I hope this activity will serve as a valuable tool in your arsenal.

SUMMARY

As we summarize this chapter, let's look back and find that serenity within the lessons we've learned.

We found our Lauren in a situation where she absolutely could not say 'no'. Now, I know Lauren's situation may seem extreme, and her cultural background might be different from yours but, honestly, haven't you found yourself in a similar position at times? Buried under the weight of others' expectations, forgetting that it's okay to say 'no'?

See, Lauren's story isn't just about her. It's about every mom who's ever felt stretched too thin, who's felt guilty for wanting to prioritize herself. It's about finding the strength to draw boundaries, to say that crucial 'no', and to understand that it doesn't make you any less of a mom, wife, or woman.

As we segue into the conclusion, let's reflect on this path and the lessons it has given us.

Lauren is an incredible woman balancing numerous roles - a mother of three, a wife, and a daughter-in-law - all under one roof. Sharing her space and life with an extended family, Lauren often struggles to say 'no' amidst cultural expectations and a demanding family. Her story might echo many of yours. Let's look at Lauren's challenges through the lens of our path and explore potential solutions.

1. Recognizing the Problem

Lauren's situation is challenging but not uncommon, particularly in cultures where extended families live together and tradition plays a key role in defining responsibilities.

- *Understanding Her Role*: Being a people pleaser, Lauren often takes on tasks that overextend her capabilities. From caring for her kids, managing household chores, and attending to her extended family's needs, she does it all. But she's left with no time for herself, and it's starting to overwhelm her.

2. Applying the Principles of Boundary Setting

Let's apply the principles we've been discussing to help Lauren:

- *Identifying Likes and Dislikes*: Lauren needs to start by reflecting on what she enjoys doing and what feels burdensome. Maybe she loves cooking but dislikes the expectation of cleaning up after everyone. Identifying these aspects can help her clarify her boundaries.

- *Expressing Boundaries Respectfully*: Once Lauren understands her boundaries, she needs to articulate them. For example, she could say, "I enjoy preparing meals for the family, but I feel overwhelmed with all the cleaning afterward. Could we establish a schedule to share this responsibility?"

3. Learning to Say 'No'

Lauren's path also involves learning to assertively, yet respectfully, say 'no.'

- *Taking Small Steps*: Saying 'no' can be challenging, especially when you're not used to it. Lauren could start small. Maybe she could decline an additional task when she's already busy with her kids' homework.
- *Releasing Guilt*: It's crucial for Lauren to let go of the guilt associated with saying 'no.' By doing so, she's not being disrespectful but she is taking care of her mental and physical wellbeing.

Lauren's story is a reflection of countless individuals across the globe juggling multiple roles in their personal and professional lives. And like her, you might also feel overwhelmed at times. But remember, as we've been exploring, it's possible to navigate these situations by setting boundaries, learning to say 'no,' and freeing yourself from guilt.

WORKSHEET

Exercises:

1. Identify a recent situation where you had difficulty saying 'no'.

Notes:

---

2. Reflect on your current boundaries: Are they healthy or unhealthy? How do they affect your relationships and your time management?

Notes:

---

3. Why do you think it's important to set boundaries and learn to say 'no'?

Notes:

---

4. Think of a turning point in your life similar to Lauren's. How did it impact you?

Notes:

5. What are some ways you can set boundaries respectfully?

Notes:

Practice Questions:

1. What do you fear most about saying 'no'?

2. In what areas of your life do you struggle with setting boundaries?

3. How has the inability to say 'no' affected your life?

4. What strategies can you implement to deal with people who don't respect your boundaries?

5. How can you create new lifestyle habits to maintain your boundaries?

Frequently Asked Questions:

1. What if setting boundaries damages my relationships?

2. How can I ensure my boundaries are respected?

3. Can boundaries change over time?

4. Is it selfish to put my needs first by setting boundaries?

5. How do I deal with guilt when saying 'no'?

Table: Identify Areas of Life

Current boundaries	Healthy boundaries	Steps to implement

Key Takeaways:

1. The power of 'no' and its role in managing personal and professional commitments.

Notes:

2. The importance of setting healthy boundaries in preserving one's mental and emotional wellbeing.

Notes:

_____

_____

3. The consequences of neglecting personal boundaries and constantly saying 'yes'.

Notes:

_____

_____

4. The role of personal transformation in setting and maintaining boundaries.

Notes:

_____

_____

5. Strategies for establishing and upholding boundaries even when they are challenged.

Notes:

_____

_____

Action Steps:

1. Identify a situation this week where you can practice saying 'no'.

_____

_____

2. Create a plan for establishing healthy boundaries in one area of your life.

_____

_____

3. Practice a conversation where you set a boundary with someone who typically disregards it.

_____

_____

4. Reflect daily on your progress in setting boundaries and saying 'no'.

_____

_____

5. Seek support or guidance if you struggle to set boundaries or say 'no'.

_____

_____

6

CREATING NEW LIFE HABITS IN ANY AREA OF YOUR LIFE

"Change might not be fast, and it isn't always easy. But with time and effort, almost any habit can be reshaped."

— CHARLES DUHIGG

I believe this quote by Charles Duhigg starting our final chapter is a perfect way to wrap up the entire book, which, at its core, is about a change, lots of changes, in fact, changes in mentality, changes in behavior, in our attitudes, pain points and our ideas about time management in general. The previous chapters taught us about time management problems and equipped us with tangible solutions, exercises, charts, and resources to overcome them. In this chapter, let's talk a bit about making changes in our habits and how to make them stick.

Making a change isn't always a walk in the park, is it? We've all been there, trying to stick to that new diet, declutter our space, or limit our screen time, only to find our old patterns creeping back. Fret not! You're not alone; the good news is that there are effective strategies to make new habits last. So, let's power up and zoom into this new chapter!

The basic structure of habit-forming can be described in three words: Cue, Routine, Reward. To instill a new habit, identify a cue (a trigger for the behavior), followed by the routine (the behavior itself), and then the reward (the benefit you gain from the behavior). Let's say you're working on saying 'no' more often. Your cue could be feeling overwhelmed by constant demand to please others; your new routine would be to assertively say 'no,' when the request or suggestion does not satisfy you or make you happy, and your reward is the freedom and time you gain to focus on your priorities.

I understand developing new habits can be very challenging and even a struggle, but remember, with the right mindset, you can increase the chances of making the new habits stick.

Here are some strategies to help you on this path:

- *Set Clear and Achievable Goals*: Define what habit you want to develop and why this particular habit is vital to you. We tend to have a better direction and motivation when having a clear objective on the horizon. Let's say you want to start taking fitness classes; picture yourself as a fit, toned woman with better metabolism and stamina, and keep this picture in mind whenever you hesitate to sign up for the next class. If you're trying to incorporate exercise into your daily routine, don't jump straight into a high-intensity workout regimen. Start with light exercises and gradually increase your intensity and duration.

- *Focus on one habit at a time.* If our habit goals are too ambitious, simultaneously aiming for too many changes can be overwhelming and intimidating. By trying to achieve ten habits at once within a short period, you may be setting yourself up for failure. Pick one habit that resonates with your current needs and wishes the most, and focus on it for a week or a month. Forming a habit may take different time frames from person to person; there is no one-size-fits-all time frame here. Some people are better suited to habit forming than others, and if you are one of the latter, that's ok. Stick to your goals and remember, "You can do it!".
- *Set small goals and achieve more:* Begin with a habit that is easy to incorporate into your daily routine. Starting with a small and achievable goal increases the likelihood of success and builds momentum. Let's say you are trying to declutter your home and put it off because the load seems too overwhelming. Don't aim to tidy up the entire house in one day. Start small, maybe with one drawer or one corner of a room. Celebrate small victories to fuel your motivation!
- *Be consistent:* Consistency is critical when developing new habits. Commit to practicing the new habit daily or on specific days if it's not a daily habit. Consistency will make it easier to stick with the new habit over time.

If you think consistency is not something that can stick with you, consider setting reminders: alarms, notifications, or visual cues will prompt you to perform the habit. You may want to start your day with a morning meditation, but instead, reach out for your phone first thing in the morning? Make a sticky note, for instance, "I start every morning with a meditation," and stick it to your night table or anywhere else where you will see it first thing in the morning. Reminders serve as triggers and help you remember to follow through with the desired habit.

- *Routine is Your Best Friend*: the key to a new habit sticking is incorporating it into your daily routine. For example, if you want to develop a daily reading habit, you can associate it with your morning coffee or evening bath. This association makes remembering and incorporating the new behavior into your life easier. Suppose you're trying to reduce screen time. Designate tech-free zones or periods during your day—for instance, no gadgets at the dinner table or an hour before bed. Consistency and repetition will help cement the habit.

- *Be patient and reap the rewards*: Building new habits takes time and effort, so what if we offer ourselves a reward like kindness? Be patient with yourself and understand that it's normal to face setbacks along the way. If you miss a day or slip up, don't be too harsh on yourself. Instead, recommit to the habit and keep moving forward, be patient and kind to yourself. Acknowledging your progress and rewarding yourself when you reach certain milestones can boost your motivation and make the habit-building process more enjoyable. You may reward yourself on a weekly or monthly basis depending on your needs and challenges. Let yourself celebrate your success.

Remember, creating new lifestyle habits is like embarking on an exciting path, and the road to success is not always a straight line. There might be bumps, turns, and setbacks along the way. But as we've learned, consistency, patience, and gradual change are the keys to successfully navigating this path of integrating new habits into your life.

PAY IT FORWARD

As your masterpiece comes together and you carve out time for yourself as well as every demand life throws at you, you put yourself in a unique position to help other people like you.

Simply by sharing your honest opinion of this book and a little about your own experience, you'll show other moms where they can find everything they need to improve their own time management skills.

Thank you so much for your support. I wish you the best of luck going forward.

CONCLUSION

As Thomas Edison once said, "Time is really the only capital that any human being has, and the only thing he can't afford to lose."

Time, the most elusive yet precious commodity in our lives, is especially valuable for mothers. Our everyday reality is a whirl-wind of tasks, responsibilities, decision-making, and occasional moments of joy and peace. We find ourselves on this shared path, weaving our paths through chaos and tranquility.

Throughout this venture, we've met five wonderful women - Emily, Sarah, Jessica, Megan, and Lauren. Each of them shared their struggles and victories, their trials and triumphs. From Emily's tech addiction to Sarah's battle with clutter, from Jessica's struggle to prioritize to Megan's overwhelming desire to do it all, and finally, Lauren's challenge with boundaries. Their stories have been our guides, our beacons of hope, our reminders that, yes, we can conquer chaos, maximize productivity, balance our schedule, and reclaim our 'me' moments.

So, what have we learned from their experiences?

Firstly, technology, a double-edged sword, can either be a friend or an enemy. The trick is to use it to our advantage, just as Emily did. From a tool of distraction, she transformed it into a tool of connection and productivity.

Secondly, the physical clutter that fills our spaces often mirrors the mental clutter crowding our minds. Sarah taught us that decluttering isn't a one-time affair. It's a process, a venture of letting go and making space for new and better things physically and emotionally.

Thirdly, priorities. Jessica reminded us of the importance of aligning our actions with our true values. To live our best lives, we must honor what truly matters to us and let those priorities guide our decisions.

Fourthly, the myth of doing it all. Megan's burnout was a harsh reality check. We learned from her experience that delegation is not a sign of weakness but a strategy for balance and sustainability.

And finally, Lauren, who showed us the power of setting boundaries and the art of saying 'no.' Her story was a testament that setting boundaries is not an act of selfishness but an essential step towards self-care and mental wellbeing.

Every story is a slice of reality, every struggle a common thread weaving us together. Each of these women discovered, in their unique ways, that managing time isn't about cramming more tasks into the day. It's about making conscious choices of where and how we spend our time.

Picture the women who mastered time management, having applied the best principles from each chapter. This woman is productive and efficient, happy and content, she serves as an inspiration to others, showcasing the benefits of effective time management and encouraging those around her to develop similar skills.

Find this woman in YOU, a mom who not only manages to balance her professional career and family life but also finds time for self-care and personal growth. You have successfully transformed your life by incorporating the strategies and tools we've explored. Your story gives us hope and encourages us to believe in our capacity for change.

If a mental picture of this woman resonates with you, now, it's your turn. The baton is in your hands. You've seen the venture unfold, the tools at your disposal, and the transformations that are possible. What step will you take today to start reclaiming your time? Remember, every small change makes a big difference. The power is in your hands.

And once you've started making these changes, I'd love to hear about your venture. Share your stories, your successes, and even your struggles. Your experiences can inspire and motivate others in this shared venture. And if you've found this book helpful, do consider leaving a review. It would mean the world to me and to others who might benefit from these insights.

In the end, remember: time is not just a sequence of moments. It's a canvas, and you're the artist. Paint it with colors of joy, strokes of fulfillment, and shades of peace. After all, you're not just managing time; you're crafting a life. Happy crafting!

By Julia Ray

REFERENCES

BOOKS

Allen, D. (2001). Getting things done: The art of stress-free productivity. New York: Penguin.

Bennett, P. (2010). Time management for the creative person. New York: Crown Business.

Covey, S. R. (1989). The 7 habits of highly effective people. New York: Free Press.

Egan, G. (2007). Work-life balance: How to convert professional success into personal happiness. Amherst, MA: HRD Press.

Kondo, M. (2014). The life-changing magic of tidying up: The Japanese art of decluttering and organizing. Tokyo: Sunmark Publishing, Inc.

Morgenstern, J. (2004). Time management from the inside out. New York: Holt Paperbacks.

Newport, C. (2016). Deep work: Rules for focused success in a distracted world. New York: Grand Central Publishing.

Sandberg, S. (2013). Lean in: Women, work, and the will to lead. New York: Knopf.

Sinek, S. (2011). Start with why: How great leaders inspire everyone to take action. London: Portfolio Penguin.

Vanderkam, L. (2018). Off the clock: Feel less busy while getting more done. New York: Portfolio.

JOURNALS

Bélanger, L., Boudrias, J. S., & Rousseau, V. (2019). The impact of goal orientation dispositions on the psychological health of leaders: An empirical study among Canadian health care professionals. Canadian Journal of Behavioural Science/Revue canadienne des sciences du comportement, 51(2), 131-141.

Clark, M. A., Michel, J. S., Zhdanova, L., Pui, S. Y., & Baltes, B. B. (2016). All work and no play? A meta-analytic examination of the correlates and outcomes of workaholism. Journal of Management, 42(7), 1836-1873.

Donnelly, G., Proctor-Thomson, S., & Jang, S. H. (2019). Workplace influences on women's work–life boundary setting and well-being. New Zealand Journal of Employment Relations, 44(1), 61-76.

Felstead, A., Henseke, G. (2017). Assessing the growth of remote working and its consequences for effort, well-being and work-life balance. New Technology, Work and Employment, 32(3), 195-212.

Kinnunen, U., Feldt, T., Siltaloppi, M., & Sonnentag, S. (2011). Job demands–resources model in the context of recovery: Testing recovery experiences as mediators. European Journal of Work and Organizational Psychology, 20(6), 805-832.

Lam, W., & Chen, Z. (2012). When I put on my service mask: Determinants and outcomes of emotional labor among hotel service providers according to affective event theory. International Journal of Hospitality Management, 31(1), 3-11.

Matthews, R. A., Barnes-Farrell, J. L., & Bulger, C. A. (2010). Advancing measurement of work and family domain boundary characteristics. Journal of Vocational Behavior, 77(3), 447-460.

Michel, A., Bosch, C., & Rexroth, M. (2014). Mindfulness as a cognitive-emotional segmentation strategy: An intervention promoting work–life balance. Journal of Occupational and Organizational Psychology, 87(4), 733-754.

Neufeind, M., O'Reilly, J., & Ranft, F. (2018). Work in the digital age. Policy Network.

Sorensen, G., Landsbergis, P., Hammer, L., Amick, B. C., Linnan, L., Yancey, A., ... & Pratt, C. (2011). Preventing chronic disease in the workplace: a workshop report and recommendations. American Journal of Public Health, 101(S1), S196-S207.

James, S. J. (2012). Charles Duhigg: The Power of Habit: Why we do what we do in life and business. Journal of Child and Family Studies, 22(4), 582–584. https://doi.org/10.1007/s10826-012-9645-6

WEBSITES

A quote by Maya Angelou. (n.d.). https://www.goodrcads.com/quotes/ 706432-each-time-a-woman-stands-up-for-herself-without-knowing

Wikipedia contributors. (2022). Allen Saunders. *Wikipedia.* https://en.wiki pedia.org/wiki/Allen_Saunders

Shubham. (2022). Time is what we want most, but what we use worst. *Epic Quotes.* https://www.epicquotes.com/time-is-what-we-want-most-but-what-we-use-worst/

Ecclesiastes 3:1-11 There is a time for everything, and a season for every activity under the heavens: a time to be born and a time to die, a time to plant and a time to uproot, a time to kill and a time to heal, a time | New International Version (NIV) | Download The Bible App Now. (n.d.). YouVersion | the Bible App | Bible.com. https://www.bible.com/bible/111/ECC.3.1-11.NIV

Author of Deep Work, Study Hacks Blog - Cal Newport. (2023, March 2). Cal Newport. https://calnewport.com/

Bryant, J. (2016). Jim Rohn Quotes That Inspire. *Self-Made Success.* https://self madesuccess.com/jim-rohn-quotes/

Lynchburg Internet Addiction Counseling | Thriveworks. (2022, February 22). Thriveworks. https://thriveworks.com/lynchburg-counseling/internet-addiction-counseling/

Staff, S. (2019). 10 Inspiring Quotes on Innovation. *SUCCESS.* https://www. success.com/10-inspiring-quotes-on-innovation/

Daily, M. F. (2016, August 20). *Inspiring Chinese Proverb – The Best Time To Plant A Tree Was 20 Years Ago, The Second Best Time Is Now - Mind Fuel Daily.* Mind Fuel Daily. https://www.mindfueldaily.com/livewell/inspiring-chinese-proverb/

McGrath, C. (2015, June 1). *Minimal Challenge - The Merrythought.* The Merrythought. https://themerrythought.com/dwelling/minimal-challenge/

Poplin, J. (2022). 37 Quotes About Decluttering to Motivate You to Live With Less. *The Simplicity Habit.* https://www.thesimplicityhabit.com/quotes-about-decluttering/

Kruse, K. (2012, July 17). Stephen Covey: 10 Quotes That Can Change Your Life. *Forbes.* https://www.forbes.com/sites/kevinkruse/2012/07/16/the-7-habits/?sh=48fb8ac039c6

Mink, M. (2021). Action Expresses Priorities. Driven Woman. https://driven-woman.com/blog/archive/action-expresses-priorities/

Salao, C. (2022). Eat the Frog: How to Boost Your Productivity. *TCK Publishing*. https://www.tckpublishing.com/eat-the-frog/

Staff, L. (2023). 160+ Famous Inspirational Quotes to Ignite the Spark in You. *LoveToKnow*. https://www.lovetoknow.com/quotes-quips/inspirational/famous-inspirational-quotes

Sharing the wit and wisdom of Mama Bombeck. (2019, May 13). *tribtoday.com*. https://www.tribtoday.com/life/burtseyeview/2019/05/sharing-the-wit-and-wisdom-of-mama-bombeck/

Direction Psychology. (2020, December 2). *You can't pour from an empty cup. . . - Direction Psychology*. https://www.directionpsychology.com/article/you-cant-pour-from-an-empty-cup/

Pierce, K. P. (2020). Almost Everything Will Work Again if You Unplug It... *The MRP Project*. https://themrpproject.org/almost-everything-will-work-again-if-you-unplug-it/

Happy No-Vember – North Country Hospital. (2021, November 4). https://www.northcountryhospital.org/healthy_you/happy-no-vember/

Horner, K. (2021). A healthy dose of "no" — courage to caregivers. *Courage to Caregivers*. https://www.couragetocaregivers.org/blogentries/2020/7/8/a-healthy-dose-of-no

Prete, A., & Prete, A. (2021). Daring to set boundaries . . . | Knot + Clover. *Knot + Clover | Therapy for Women*. https://knotandclover.com/daring-to-set-boundaries-is-about-having-the-courage-to-love-ourselves-even-when-we-risk-disappointing-others/

Power, R. (2021, January 5). 3 things ultra productive people do differently. *Inc.com*. https://www.inc.com/rhett-power/3-things-ultra-productive-people-do-differently_1.html

Shah, M. (2022, March 29). *The bad news is time flies. The good news is you're the pilot*. SetQuotes. https://www.setquotes.com/the-bad-news-is-time-flies-the-good-news-is-youre-the-pilot/

Printed in Great Britain
by Amazon